VILLAGE GOVERNMENT IN BRITISH INDIA

VILLAGE GOVERNMENT IN BRITISH INDIA

JOHN MATTHAI

GYAN

Published by

GYAN

Gyan Publishing House
5, Ansari Road
Daryaganj, New Delhi-110002
Phone: 011-47034999, 9811692060
E-mail: books@gyanbooks.com

Distribution Network
gyanbooks.com
India, USA, Canada, UK, Australia

ISBN: 978-93-7014-549-8 (PB)

First Published, 1915

2nd Impression 2025

Printed at: Gyan Press, Delhi.

VILLAGE GOVERNMENT IN BRITISH INDIA
Author: JOHN MATTHAI

VILLAGE GOVERNMENT IN BRITISH INDIA

VILLAGE GOVERNMENT IN BRITISH INDIA

BY

JOHN MATTHAI

SOMETIME TUTOR IN HISTORY, MADRAS CHRISTIAN COLLEGE;
"VAKĪL" OF THE HIGH COURT OF JUDICATURE, MADRAS

WITH A PREFACE

BY

SIDNEY WEBB

PROFESSOR OF PUBLIC ADMINISTRATION,
UNIVERSITY OF LONDON

LONDON

T. FISHER UNWIN, LTD.

ADELPHI TERRACE

AUTHOR'S PREFACE

THE object of this preface is simply to acknowledge obligations. My chief debt is to the Professor of Public Administration for his interest in this study and for the great help which I have derived from his extensive knowledge of the ideas and machinery of Local Government. My next obligation is to the Librarian of the India Office and his staff for the abundant facilities which they gave me for access to books and records, and for their kindness and courtesy during the two years I worked there. Among those who have been good enough to help me with suggestions and criticism, I must mention especially Mr. S. C. Hill, late Superintendent of the Imperial Records Office, Calcutta; Mr. R. W. Frazer, Lecturer in Dravidian Languages at the Imperial Institute; and Mr. J. S. Cotton, Editor of the *Imperial Gazetteer of India.* On village administration in North India, of which my knowledge is to a large extent second-hand, I have had the advantage of some talks with Sir James Wilson and Sir J. M. Douie, which have been distinctly illuminating.

JOHN MATTHAI.

LONDON SCHOOL OF ECONOMICS
AND POLITICAL SCIENCE,
UNIVERSITY OF LONDON.
October 1, 1915.

PREFACE

I HOPE that this little book, which Mr. Matthai has written with so much research and insight, may open the way for many further studies on Indian Local Government.

The fragments of an indigenous Local Government that are still to be traced in Indian village life seem to me full of interest and suggestion. They are, it need hardly be said, easily overlooked. One able collector of long service in Central India informed me that he had been, until a few months before, totally unaware that anything of the sort existed in any of the villages over which he ruled. But being led to make specific inquiries on the subject, he had just discovered, in village after village, a distinctly effective, if somewhat shadowy, local organization, in one or other form of *panchayat*, which was, in fact, now and then giving decisions on matters of communal concern, adjudicating civil disputes, and even condemning offenders to reparation and fine. Such a Local Government organization is, of course, "extra-legal," and has no statutory warrant, and, in the eyes of the British tribunals, possesses no authority whatever. But it has gone on silently existing, possibly for longer than the British Empire itself, and is still effectively functioning, merely by common consent and with the very real sanction of the local public opinion. Mr. Matthai's careful descriptions enable us to realize what this Village Government has been, and probably often still is, and the subjects with which it deals.

I may perhaps be permitted to cite a similar experience of my own. In England there are about three hundred local authorities, styled Commissioners of Sewers, who have been appointed by Royal Authority, in some places for six or seven centuries, and who derive their powers to protect the land from floodings, and to tax and to fine, exclusively from Parliament and the King. Underlying these august dignitaries, however, the careful observer may discover, in one county after another, still existing fragments of another and an older local organization against floodings, unknown to the statutory constitution and never yet described in any book, in the form of juries of local residents who make their own rules, exercise their own primitive "watch and ward" of the embankments and dykes, carry out the minor precautionary measures that they themselves devise, and stand in a curious and ever-varying relationship, unprovided for by statute, to the official Commissioners, who naïvely regard themselves as the sole Local Authorities. Mr. Matthai rightly draws attention to another analogy, in the common blacksmith, the common innkeeper, the common miller, and the common carrier of rural England—immemorial village officials, bound to village service, long unknown to the lawyers of the King's Courts, and entirely unauthorized by Parliament.

One suggestion that these fragments of indigenous Indian Local Government seem to afford is that we sometimes tend to exaggerate the extent to which the cleavages of caste have prevailed over the community of neighbourhood. How often is one informed, "with authority," that the *panchayat* of which we catch glimpses must be only a caste *panchayat!* It is plain, on the evidence, that however frequent and potent may be the *panchayat* of a caste, there have been and still are *panchayats* of men of different castes, exercising the functions of a Village Council over villagers of different castes. How widely prevalent these may be not even the Government of India can yet inform us. But if people would only look for traces of Village Government, instead of mainly for evidences of caste dominance, we might learn more on the subject. Now, whatever may be the advantages of caste divisions, it is plain that they constitute, for the most part, an obstacle to the development of Government, central or local. The gradual substitution of territorial for tribal organization in Europe, which it took many centuries to accomplish, and the equally gradual supersession of family law by the law of the geographical neighbourhood, lie at the roots of European progress. Local Government, at any rate, must, to be effective, nowadays be based, in the main, not on tribal or family but on neighbourhood groups. The common services that it provides, the common rules that it enacts, and the common fund that it administers must, in practice, be those of the village or the district as a whole. Where caste lines are strong it is doubtless practically impossible to ignore them, however disastrous may be the cleavages that they cause. But we see that, even where caste exists, it has, in fact, permitted a great deal of common life, and that it is compatible with active Village Councils. It seems important, therefore, to emphasize, not to ignore, all the common life of the Indian village, in which the necessities of neighbourhood have held their own, or have prevailed against the divisions of caste.

It is not for me to dwell upon the advantage, on which various Government Resolutions and Minutes have insisted, of making use of, and developing, such fragments of indigenous Local Government as exist in India ; and of shaping the new upon the lines of the old. But I may be permitted to draw attention to the extent to which the newest thought, in France as well as in England, is emphasizing the importance of not resting content with even the best possible development of National, Provincial, or Municipal Government, organized merely "from above," in large geographical districts. What is now being urged, with convincing authority, with regard not to India but to Western Europe, is that any such government, however mechanically perfect, will fail to take root in the minds of the mass of the people—will fail to gain from them the life without which it will be but a clog upon their own development—unless it is in some way grafted on the spontaneous groupings of the people themselves, whether these be groupings by vocation or by race, by community of religious belief or by propinquity of neighbourhood ; and this however incongruous may seem the conceptions and the procedure of these spontaneous popular groupings, with the theoretical conclusions of our political science. For instance, in England as in France, we still habitually think of Democracy as being, or at least as necessarily involving, the Popular Election of representatives or rulers : the Indian village, like the Russian mir, may remind us that Vote by Ballot and Party Government are only two among several expedients for bringing administration under public control. We make much, in Western Europe and America, of Decision by Majority Vote : the Indian village offers us, like the Quaker meeting, a possibly higher alternative, if we believe in Government by Consent, in Decision by the General Sense of the Community. In England our lawyers and statesmen are still encumbered with the Austinian pedantry of a century ago, which taught them that obligations are but the obverse of rights, and that nothing is a right which is not enforceable by judicial proceedings —the inference being that there can be no binding obligation to the public at large, to the village as a whole, to the craft to which one belongs, to all the members of one's family, or to future generations. The Indian Village, like the Early English Manor, emphasizes obligations rather than rights ; and far from confining itself to rights on which some particular person could take action for his own benefit, devotes itself largely to the enforcement of obligations to the public.

If one who knows, at first hand, next to nothing about the country may be permitted any opinion at all, I would suggest that, as a factor of effective social progress in India, the development of Local Government stands second in importance to scarcely any whatsoever. The routine administration of the common affairs of the Village, the Municipality, and the District—even putting aside for the moment those of the Province ; how these are actually being organized in the different parts of India, and with what result ; the way in which more social tissue is being, or can be, developed for the communal management of the school and the temple, the relief of the helpless and distressed, the maintenance of the public health, the execution of public works and the organization of public services, the protection of life and property and the settlement of disputes—all this presents a field for study which is likely to be of real use to India ; and, indeed, to the world. We are accustomed, in Europe, to take as a rough test of the social administration of any nation the changes in its annual death-rate ; or, rather, in the average expectation of life of the whole population. The first and most important business of a Government is, after all, to contrive that its people should live and not die ! In the long run, in the judgment of history, it is by this test that Governments will be judged. How does India stand this test ? In the most civilized parts of Europe, during the past three-quarters of a century, *mainly by a development of Local Government*—using only that scientific knowledge which is equally available to all administrations—we have about doubled the average expectation of life of the whole population. Seeing that in India, where the circumstances are more adverse, the average expectation of life of the people is only somewhere about one-half that of the people of

England,[1] there is perhaps no direction in which the community could more profitably invest its thought, its effort, and its money, than in a wise development of its Local Government. I am glad to think that this idea is more and more engaging the attention of the thoughtful European or American missionary and British official. But in this as in other matters it is to India itself that, in the main, India must look; and there might with advantage be a much greater turning of attention, among Indian students and their instructors, to the problems of Local Government. I do not know how many of the couple of hundred university colleges in India have even one course of lectures each session describing the history, the organization, and the functions of Local Government in India or elsewhere. I have not heard of the foundation of any Professorship of Local Government. I wonder how many books on Local Government are to be found in the libraries to which the Indian college students have access. How often have Provincial Directors of Education called attention to this omission? It would be interesting to inquire how frequently any problem of Local Government has been given as a subject for an essay, or made the topic for discussion at a debating society.

Local Government, it is only fair to say, though as old as the hills, and a practical success for more than half a century, is a relatively new discovery to the professor of political science, as it is to the politician. Right down to the end of the nineteenth century, august treatises on the British Constitution, and solemn surveys of the functions of government, confined themselves exclusively to the organization and development of the National or Central Government, which is decorated

[1] What a loss, what a tragedy it is that so many of India's most valuable citizens die before they are fifty! A deliberate scientific investigation into the causes of premature death in India, of adults subject neither to privation nor to industrial accidents or diseases, might be of great value.

with the trappings of royalty, and made the subject of Parliamentary discussion. In common talk we followed suit, and usually refused to regard as "government" all that vast part of the governmental machinery of the community which is administered locally. We have discussed endlessly, in England as in India, the shortcomings of "the Government," and the need for its reform, in this way or that. But we do not give sufficient heed in England—and I suspect that this is even more the case in India—to that part of Government which really concerns us most, because it is merely Local Government.

This neglect is, I venture to think, a grave mistake. In the nations which, in the twentieth century, regard themselves as the most advanced in civilization, or the most highly developed in social life—whether we take the United Kingdom or Germany, France or the United States—we find that by far the largest part of government is now that which is not carried on in the capital cities, by Departments of State, at the bidding of Parliaments; but that which is being administered locally, in village or parish or commune, in municipality or county or district, by the direction and for the advantage of the people of these localities. In times of peace, indeed, Local Government has become, in these advanced countries, in the aggregate, actually more extensive than the Central or National Government; apart from the payment of interest on old debts it often spends more money and has many more officials in its employment; it usually carries on more enterprises and conducts more services for the common good; it even enacts, in its by-laws and regulations, a greater volume of laws that we have to obey than the National Legislature. This is not because Parliament has become less energetic or less important. On the contrary, it is busier and more important than ever. But the other branch of Government, Local Government, has, during the past half-century, enormously grown, so that in England all the aggregate of parish councils, district councils, borough councils, and county councils come to be, in magnitude or volume of business, greater than all the Government Departments put together. This, I apprehend, is very far from being the position in India to-day. But if India is to advance in civilization and prosperity as other countries have advanced, it seems probable that an analogous growth of Local Government—even to the extent of its doing more work, spending more money, employing more officials, and making more laws than the Viceroy and his Councils—will, in the course of the coming century, take place in India.

It has sometimes been said, as a reason why the business of government will never really enter effectively into the minds of the mass of the people of India, that they are "a people of villagers." Such a fact, as it seems to me, would be at least an argument for a great and far-reaching expansion of Village Government. But I suggest that it may not in reality be true (though non-Indians are sometimes reproached for their seeming ignorance on this point) that the people of India are a people of villagers, in the sense in which that phrase is commonly used. The Census, indeed, tells us that something like nine out of every ten of the dwellers between the Himalayas and Cape Comorin are found inhabiting villages of less than 5,000 population. But it is a mistake to assume that a land of villages necessarily means what is usually implied by the phrase, a people of villagers. In truth India, for all its villages, has been also, at all known periods, and to-day still is, perhaps to a greater extent than ever before, what Anglo-Saxon England, for instance, was not, or the South African Republic in the days before gold had been discovered, and what the Balkan Peninsula even at the present time may perhaps not be, namely, a land of flourishing cities, of a distinctly urban civilization, exhibiting not only splendid architecture, and the high development of the manufacturing arts made possible by the concentration of population and wealth, but likewise—what is much more important—a secretion of thought, an accumulation of knowledge, and a development of literature and philosophy which are not in the least like the characteristic products of villagers as we know them in Europe or America. And to-day, although the teeming crowds who throng the narrow lanes of Calcutta or Benares, Bombay or Poona, Madras or Hyderabad, or even the millions who temporarily swarm at Hardwar or Allahabad or Puri, may include only a small percentage of the whole population, yet the Indian social order does not seem to be, in the European understanding of the phrase, either on its good or on its bad side, essentially one of villagers. The distinction may be of importance, because the Local Government developed by peoples of villagers, as we know of them in Anglo-Saxon England, in the early days of the South African Republic, and in the Balkan States, is of a very different type from that which takes root and develops, even in the villages, in those nations which have also a city life, centres of religious activity, colleges and universities, and other "nodal points," from which emanate, through popular literature, pilgrimages, and the newspaper press, slow but far-spreading waves of thought and feeling, and aspirations which it is fatal to ignore. It is very largely through the development of Local Government that such a people becomes an organized nation.

It seems a pity that the aspirations of so many Indians for "Indian Self-Government," and especially those of Indian students, should contemplate so exclusively that part of Government which concerns India as a whole. After all, even in such "self-governing" Dominions as Canada and Australia, the part that is played in the government of the country by the Dominion Governor-General, the Dominion Legislature, and the Dominion Civil Service, is not by any means so large as it is conspicuous. It is the Local

Government of Village or Municipality that touches most nearly the lives of the people. It is because they themselves run their Local Government, much more than in respect of any real share that they have in the Dominion Governments, that these peoples are essentially "self-governing." I do not in any way deprecate the desire or belittle the claim that India, like other parts of the British Empire, should be administered in the main by Indians in accordance with Indian public opinion. But in India, as elsewhere, it is Local Government that is destined to grow, at a much greater rate than Central Government, and the importance of the field thus opening out should not be overlooked. There is here, as it seems to me, a greater and certainly a more accessible sphere for the exercise of autonomy. In practice it will be found, as the century advances, that by far the greater part of "Indian Self-Government," and more and more of the part in which the daily lives of the Indian people are most intimately concerned, will lie, not in the sphere of His Excellency the Viceroy in Council—not even in that of the Provincial Governments—but in those of the Village Council, the District Board, and the Municipality, or of any Local Authorities that may supersede them. In the fully organized India of a century hence, as in the England of to-morrow, it may well be that it may be these, or some analogous bodies, that will be found exercising actually the larger part of all the functions of government, expending the larger part of that share of the people's income which is administered collectively, appointing and controlling the majority of all the salaried servants of the community, and even enacting, in the aggregate, in their by-laws and regulations, a greater volume of the laws that the people obey.

SIDNEY WEBB.

41 Grosvenor Road, Westminster.
October 1915.

CONTENTS

VILLAGE GOVERNMENT IN BRITISH INDIA

CHAPTER I

INTRODUCTORY

1. THIS essay is mainly an attempt to bring together the chief facts about village local government which have been noticed in Indian official publications, especially during the past fifty years. Some very able and informing books have been written, notably by the late Sir Henry Maine and Mr. B. H. Baden-Powell, on the Indian village community as a system of landholding and economic association. It was Sir Henry Maine's work [1] which first drew the serious attention of European students to the place of the village community in the progress of society in the East and the West. His aim was not to describe the constitution of the village community in any detail, but rather by insisting on some of its broader features to show its relation to a study of early communities in general. The collection of official information in India had not proceeded very far in Maine's time; and he had to depend to a large extent on personal observation and informal reports. This necessarily left some of his data open

[1] 1. *Village Communities in the East and West*; 2. *Early History of Institutions*; 3. *Ancient Law*; 4. *Early Law and Custom.*

to question, as judged by the light of subsequent information. But it would be hardly right to say that this has in any serious measure taken away from the value of Maine's writings on the Indian village. They are still, in a real sense, the classical authority on the subject; and they are likely to remain so whatever additional information on specific questions may be brought out by future research.

2. A full and possibly exhaustive account of the village community on its economic side was produced by Mr. B. H. Baden-Powell in his two well-known books.[1] It is a detailed and accurate description of the methods of landholding met with in the various provinces of British India. As the village is still the administrative unit in revenue matters, there is necessarily a great deal of valuable information to be found in the book, on the position of the village—its officers and institutions—in the scheme of Indian administration. Baden-Powell relied mainly for his materials on the official reports of land settlement in India and on the valuable series of *District Gazetteers* in the different provinces, some of which had already been compiled and others were in process of being compiled. His book is that of a patient and careful student working upon an extensive range of materials, scattered throughout the length and breadth of the country, but accessible in a reliable and more or less definite form. His work has rather supplemented than superseded Maine; and though in certain important details his researches have shown up the defects in Maine's data, on the whole his contribution is to be regarded as filling in the comprehensive outline sketched out by Maine's master hand. The one was telescopic in his vision, the other microscopic.

3. Both these authoritative writers, however, have

[1] 1. *The Land Systems of British India.* 3 vols. Clarendon Press, 1892. 2. *The Indian Village Community.* Longmans, 1896.

to a large extent confined their attention to the village community in its relation to the holding and cultivation of land. This, of course, is the primary interest of the village community and by far the most complicated and difficult problem in connection with it. Nevertheless, it cannot but be that when a wandering tribe settles down to a stationary occupation on a definite plot of land, other interests and problems must arise besides looking after and improving the means of living. Their first concern must needs be how to till the land and make the best use of its resources, and if they have reached the stage of living under the protection of a king, to give him his dues from the produce of the land. But while these things occupy the largest amount of attention, the ordinary human relationships into which men are brought in a settled society will bring in their wake such questions as the settlement of disputes, the prevention of crime, and the improvement of the means of general well-being. In the way in which these questions are met, between the primitive village community and the most highly developed modern state, the resemblances are perhaps as striking as the differences. The object of this essay is to present a connected picture of the methods adopted by the village community to meet these simple administrative needs, *so far as they may be gathered from the relics which have survived and have been recorded.* It also aims at showing how far these simple expedients have been retained or refashioned under British rule. But it lays no claim whatever to any special understanding of the Hindu village community in its palmy days, or to having made any research in that direction.

4. It is necessary at the outset to point out some of the limits which have been set to this work. The meaning which will be given throughout to the term *Village Government* is that part of the government of a village which is carried on by means of individual

officers and public bodies exercising jurisdiction, as a rule, within the local limits of a single village. This by no means represents the whole administrative work done in a village under present conditions, for a very considerable share of the work—and often the more important—is done by means of government officers and local boards having charge of larger or smaller groups of villages. Unless this fact is remembered, the following pages will be found to provide a very one-sided picture of village administration in India. The question which it is sought to answer here is, not how a village in British India is administered, but rather in what parts of this administration and to what extent are the local officers and institutions of the village community utilized.

5. Again, this study of village government is confined to British India. That is, it excludes from its survey the Protected States and Agencies, what are called the Native States. This, even in point of sheer magnitude, is to make a considerable deduction, because while the area enclosed within the geographical boundaries of India is about 1,800,000 square miles inhabited by more than 300,000,000 people, the area covered in the Native States is about 824,000 square miles and the population 70,000,000.[1] But the extent of the deduction is more than merely numerical. It is probable that in the Native States where archaic institutions possess on the whole a more sheltered life, the old village institutions will be found in a less disorganized form than in British India. To exclude the Native States, then, is to exclude what is possibly a more fruitful field of study from our point of view. But this has been thought necessary, partly for reducing the compass of the survey, there being much greater diversity in the

[1] *Imperial Gazetteer of India*, vol. iv, pp. 59, 61.

Native States than in the provinces of British India; and partly because of the comparative absence of reliable recorded materials in the vast majority of the Native States.

6. A third limitation is the exclusion from this essay of the whole subject of land revenue and the allied subject of the rights of a village community in adjacent forests. In the administration of land revenue, village communities and officers play an important part, both in the collection of the taxes and in maintaining the necessary accounts. This, in fact, is their most important share in village administration. Every other thing they do comes a long way behind in importance. The subject, however, is dealt with in such detail in Baden-Powell's book[1] that it is profitless to attempt a less full and clear account here. Besides, the subject of land revenue in India is so enormously complex that on a short and second-hand study it seems much the safer thing, in spite of its obvious disadvantages, to leave the subject alone as far as possible. The other question, namely, that of giving village communities the right to cut fuel and graze cattle in neighbouring forest areas and to make their own arrangements for enjoying the right, has often engaged the attention of provincial governments. Recently the Madras Government took steps to organize village forest committees in selected areas. But the whole matter remains more or less tentative.

7. The importance of the village in Indian administration consists in the fact that the vast majority of the inhabitants still live in villages. It is difficult to lay down precisely the distinction between a town and a village in India, though to an observer on the spot the distinction may appear fairly easy. Some rough idea of the difference may be got by

[1] *The Land Systems of British India.*

following the Census definition of the terms "town" and "village." A town was held to include—

(1) Every Municipality.
(2) All Civil Lines not included within Municipal limits.
(3) Every Cantonment.
(4) Every other continuous collection of houses inhabited by not less than 5,000 persons, which the Provincial Superintendent (of Census operations) may decide to treat as a town for Census purposes.

Of these (2) and (3) are of relatively little consequence and may safely be left out of account. The two main factors, then, which according to the Census standard determine whether a locality is a town or a village are: (1) whether a Municipal Council has been set up in the locality, and (2) whether the population exceeds 5,000. With regard to the former, there is a provision in most provinces against the introduction of Municipal Councils in areas in which a large proportion of the population depend on agriculture for their subsistence. Therefore, the chief distinction between a place which possesses a Municipal Council and one which does not is that the first is mainly industrial, while the second is mainly agricultural. This, though on the whole true, must be taken with a considerable degree of qualification. With regard to the second, namely, the standard of population, it has been urged that the minimum of 5,000 fixed for an Indian town is too high. The following comment on the point in the last Census Report is instructive. "In Germany 'landstädte' or places with a population of 2,000 to 5,000 are included in the urban category; in America the same category is used to include all 'incorporated' places with a population of 2,500 and upwards, and in England all sanitary districts with

3,000 or more inhabitants. In fixing the standard for India at 5,000, however, we have certainly not erred in the direction of over-exclusiveness. The local conditions are wholly different from those prevailing in Western countries; and the great majority of places with that number of inhabitants, whether municipalities or not, partake rather of the nature of overgrown villages than of towns as the term is understood in Europe. Trade and industry are still to a great extent monopolized by the larger towns. With the spread of railways and the general improvement in means of communication, the smaller towns are growing in importance as distributing centres, but the process is a slow one and comparatively little progress in this direction has yet been made." [1]

8. Understanding a village in this sense, it will be found that there is a fairly uniform distribution of population between towns and villages in the different provinces of British India. The proportion who live in villages varies from about 85 to 95 per cent. The general rate of distribution for the whole of India per thousand of population is as follows:—

	Villages.	Towns.
British India	905	95
Native States	900	100

If we divide villages into four classes, as below, according to the number of inhabitants: (1) over 5,000, (2) from 2,000 to 5,000, (3) from 500 to 2,000, (4) under 500—we get the following distribution for every thousand of the village population:—

	5,000 and over.	2,000 to 5,000	500 to 2,000	Under 500.
British India	18	138	483	360
Native States	10	114	454	422 [2]

[1] *Census of India*, 1911, vol. i, part i, p. 29. [2] *Ibid.*, p. 52, table iv.

9. It must not be assumed that in all the areas noted as villages in the Census Report, there were in existence in the past village communities in the sense of close corporations of agriculturists living a more or less common life. It is true that the village community must have existed in some form or other in nearly every part of India; and evidences of its survival are still found, though less easily distinguishable in some places than in others. There are certain regions, however, where the system of village communities does not appear to have existed at all. And, therefore, when we speak of village local government here, we mean what is almost entirely an artificial creation. Whatever local unity there is in these places is the result of the new administrative machinery. Three such areas have been noted. First, the British Himalayan districts which contain a limited area of flat land and occasional patches of good soil on the hill-side. People live here in single homesteads or in very small groups of two or three families.[1] Secondly, along the west coast towards the south—the districts of North Kanara, South Kanara, and Malabar—the land here lying between the sea and the Western Ghat mountains is constantly intersected by hills and rivers and wide ravines. The inhabitants generally live in isolated homesteads, each with its own garden.[2] Thirdly, the districts in the South Punjab below Multan where the country is so rainless that permanent cultivation is possible only under exceptional circumstances.[3] To these may be added the tract of country along the North-West Frontier—Baluchistan, the North-West Frontier Province, and parts of Sind—where society is still organized in tribal rather than in village communities. The introduction of settled administration has tended to the formation

[1] *The Indian Village Community*, Baden-Powell, Longmans, 1896, p. 57.
[2] *Ibid.*, p. 62. [3] *Ibid.*, p. 64.

of villages as local units. But whenever the term "village" is used, it must be understood to mean little more than the administrative area occupied by a subdivision of a tribe and does not necessarily connote any settled corporate life.

10. The systems of landholding met with in village communities in different parts of India show an immense variety of principle as well as detail. But amid all this extraordinary diversity, two main types may be distinguished with a certain degree of clearness. They have been called respectively the Landlord and the Non-Landlord type. The former is met with in the Punjab, the United Provinces, and the greater part of the Central Provinces, while the latter is found principally in Madras and Bombay and, we may add, Burma. The characteristic of the Landlord village is that there is in it a powerful joint body of proprietors who form a close oligarchy in relation to the general mass of inhabitants. They claim jointly the entire village site, the cultivated land and the waste; and the other inhabitants pay rents to them for permission to hold and use land. Here the revenue was formerly assessed on the village as a whole, and the incidence was distributed among the members of the proprietary group. In the Non-Landlord village there is no joint ownership and no communal responsibility for paying the revenue. Each cultivator holds his own land and pays the tax on it directly to the State. According to Baden-Powell, the difference between the two types may possibly be traced to their respective origins. In the first case, it may be inferred that the village community was founded either (*a*) by a body of men knit together by ties of blood or association who originally colonized the village or conquered it—or (*b*) by a single proprietor who obtained the village by grant or purchase. In the second case, the village was probably founded by individual settlers clearing the jungle, each for himself, a bit here and a bit

there, sufficient to satisfy the separate needs of each settler.[1]

11. The differences between the two types of villages need not detain us here, because so far as the administrative system is concerned, the differences, though great, do not call for a separate treatment of the two types. The main contrast in point of local administration appears to lie in the relative importance assigned to the village headman under the two systems. In villages of the Non-Landlord class, where there is a large mass of smallholders of equal position and influence, it becomes sooner or later necessary to appoint a single leader and to entrust him with sufficient powers to keep the community together. In the other class, a close oligarchy of large proprietors do not lie under the same necessity to secure the services of a common chief. And besides, the mutual jealousies which arise in such a narrow circle would render a choice difficult even if the necessity were proved. The result is that in the former, the headman has always been part of the original constitution, holding an important position in every sphere of village life, while in the latter the headman is a comparatively recent creation of Government and the original purpose of his appointment was simply to act as an intermediary in revenue matters between the proprietary body and the Government.[2]

12. It is perhaps superfluous to seek for any deeper explanation of the origin of village communities than the necessity for combination in order to satisfy certain elementary needs. The principal need was probably that of mutual defence against different kinds of adverse forces. To men settled in a dense jungle the greatest danger might arise from wild beasts and plundering

[1] *Land Systems of British India*, Baden-Powell, vol. i, pp. 144-54. Maine's ideas of the Indian village were probably derived altogether from the Landlord type of village.

[2] The term "Lambardar" used to denote a headman in a Landlord village means really one who bears a number, the number relsting to the register of village landholders in the collector's office.

tribesmen, while to those living in an open country, the danger might arise from other groups of men like themselves. And then when a tract of country is settled and brought under the authority of a central power, there comes the need of meeting the demands of the king's revenue agents. Each common need of this sort, we may suppose, would furnish an incentive to unite. In his book, *The Economic Transition in India*,[1] Sir Theodore Morison points out the analogy in this respect between the village communities of India and of France—an analogy which perhaps will hold good between village communities everywhere. While this sense of some strong common need must have been the prevailing cause, we may also believe that whenever a wandering tribe settled down, the mere tribal instinct of association would lead to the formation of compact groups, apart from any pressing necessity for combination.[2]

13. In addition to these causes, we find that under ordered and centralized governments, the king himself might originate and direct the formation of new village communities. In the *Arthaśāstra*, an ancient Indian political treatise commonly ascribed to the time of the Emperor Chandragupta Maurya[3] (d. 297 B.C.), the following reference occurs to new villages: "Either by inducing foreigners to immigrate or by causing the thickly populated centres of his own kingdom to send forth the excessive population, the king may construct villages either on new sites or on old ruins. Villages consisting each of not less than 100 families and of not more than 500 families of agricultural people of the Sudra caste, with boundaries extending as far as a *krosa* (900 feet) or two, and capable of protecting each other shall be formed.

[1] Murray, 1911, pp. 35–6.

[2] *Land Systems of British India*, Baden-Powell, vol. i, p. 108.

[3] "We may accept it (the *Arthaśāstra*) as an authoritative account of political and social conditions in the Gangetic plain in the age of Alexander the Great, 325 B.C."—*Early History of India*, V. A. Smith, Oxford, 1914, pp. 136–7.

Boundaries shall be denoted by a river, a mountain, forests, bulbous plants, caves, artificial buildings (*sētubandha*), or by trees."[1]

14. A similar instance of the king taking the initiative in the formation of a village community appears in a South Indian inscription of the thirteenth century A.D. The village in question was intended to accommodate 108 Brahmans. Sufficient land was purchased for the village site, which was to contain room for the erection of a temple, and for the house-sites of the 108 Brahmans, of the village servants and of the men in charge of the village library (*Sarasvatī-Bhāndhārattar*). The lands were bought from the old title-holders and tenants with all the benefits and appurtenances which belonged to them; and these were transferred in their entirety to the new settlers. A right of way was secured over certain lands outside the village for the Brahmans to walk to the tank for the performance of the daily prayers (*Sandhyā Vandana*). Land was also provided for grazing cattle, for the maintenance of the families of the new settlers, each of whom appears to have received a definite piece of land, and for the remuneration of the village officers and artisans.[2]

15. It is probably to artificial villages of this kind which were established under the direction of the king that the detailed regulations for planning and building villages, laid down in the *Manasara Silpasastra*[3] would be found to apply. There is an interesting summary of these regulations in a recent book by Mr. E. B. Havell, *Ancient and Medieval Architecture of India.*[4] Elaborate rules are laid down for the selection of a

---

[1] *Mysore Review*, February 1907.

[2] *Madras Epigraphy*, *Annual Report*, 1913–14, p. 92.

[3] An architectural treatise "stated to be the production of a sage named Mānasāra and of great celebrity in the south of India as affording copious information on every branch of the art on which he treats." *Essay on the Architecture of the Hindus*, Rām Rāz, London, 1834, p. 3.

[4] Murray, 1915, pp. 4–15.

proper site, for the alignment and construction of streets, and for the erection of houses and public buildings. But it must of course be unsafe to infer that these rules represent the general condition of Indian villages at the time. If we take any particular kingdom built by conquest, as most of these kingdoms must have been, it must be very difficult to say how many of the villages, if any, were built newly on the plans of the *Silpasastra* and how many had been there already in the more or less primitive and diversified condition of naturally formed village communities. It seems reasonable to suggest, in the absence of stronger evidence to the contrary, that even in the most highly developed kingdom, the latter class of villages must have far exceeded the former in numbers. Mr. Havell's statement, in speaking of the King's Highway in the Empire of Chandragupta Maurya, that it linked together "the hundreds of single villages planned on the principles of the *Silpasastras* which lay between the seat of the central government and the farthest confines of the Empire,"[1] however attractive, seems somewhat wide.

16. The formation of new village communities has proceeded in India even in our own time. A remarkable instance is the Canal Colonies of the Punjab, where immense tracts of waste land have been brought under irrigation and rendered cultivable. These are settlements of peasant lessees, to a large extent resembling the Non-Landlord type of villages. Their holdings are "Crown tenancies" without rights of transfer; and of late years there has been a not imperceptible growth of communal feeling among them. Somewhat similar are the experiments in village settlement which have been carried on in recent years by the Church Missionary Society in parts of Bengal and the United Provinces. One of their most success-

[1] P. 25.

ful efforts has been the settlement of a colony of Santal Christians in Jalpaiguri in Eastern Bengal. The present area of the colony is about 14 square miles. It is divided into ten villages, each of which has a headman chosen by the villagers and appointed by the superintending missionary. The affairs of the colony are managed by a council presided over by the Indian pastor, of which the headmen are members. The people have built their own school-house and church, and pay their own teachers. At present there are about 1,500 Christian and 500 other colonists. "Those who are not Christians sign a pledge to abstain from intoxicating drink and heathen sacrifices and to abide by the rules of the colony." [1]

17. It may be useful in an account of village institutions to add a description of the external features presented by a modern Indian village. But to attempt such a description would be to presuppose a uniformity of appearance which does not exist in actual fact. Not merely between one province and another, but sometimes even within the area of a single district, differences are met with which render fanciful the idea of a single uniform type. So far as it is possible to form a picture by piecing together a few outstanding common features, the following brief description in the *Imperial Gazetteer of India* [2] will be found to be a true portraiture. "The typical Indian village has its central residential site, with an open space for a pond and a cattle stand. Stretching around this nucleus lie the village lands, consisting of a cultivated area and (very often) grounds for grazing and woodcutting. The arable lands have their several boundary marks, and their little subdivisions of earth ridges made for retaining rain or irrigation water. The inhabitants of such a village pass their life in the midst of these simple surroundings,

[1] *Eastern Bengal District Gazetteers*, Jalpaiguri, pp. 44–5. [2] Vol. vi, p. 279.

welded together in a little community with its own organization and government, which differ in character in the various types of villages, its body of detailed customary rules, and its little staff of functionaries, artisans, and traders."

18. The "staff of functionaries, artisans, and traders" by means of which village communities carried on their internal government have survived in a recognizable form almost everywhere. A list of officers and public servants in a Madras village at the beginning of last century is contained in a report of a Select Committee of the House of Commons, issued in 1812, commonly known as the *Fifth Report.*[1]

The *headman*, who has the general superintendence of the affairs of the village, settles the disputes of the inhabitants, attends to the police, and performs the duty of collecting the revenues within his village.

The *accountant*, who keeps the accounts of cultivation and registers everything connected with it.

The *watchmen*, of whom there are two kinds—the superior and inferior. The duty of the former is to gain information of crimes and offences and to escort and protect persons travelling from one village to another. The province of the latter is more immediately confined to the village, consisting among other duties in guarding the crops and assisting in measuring them.

The *boundaryman*, who preserves the limits of the village or gives evidence respecting them in cases of dispute.

The *superintendent of the tanks and water-courses* distributes the water therefrom for the purposes of agriculture.

The *priest*, who performs the village worship.

The *schoolmaster*, who is seen teaching the children in the villages to read and write in the sand.

[1] Parliamentary Paper, 1812 (377), vii, 1, pp. 84–5.

The *astrologer*, who proclaims the lucky or unpropitious periods for sowing and threshing.

The *smith* and *carpenter*, who manufacture the implements of agriculture and build the dwellings of the ryot.

The *potter*.

The *washerman*.

The *barber*.

The *cowkeeper*.

The *doctor*.

The *dancing-girl*.

The *musician and poet*.

19. The village artisans mentioned in this list may be taken as fairly typical of the greater part of the country.[1] It is practically, though not wholly, identical with the more recent descriptions of village services which occur in the *District Gazetteers* of the various provinces.[2] In South, and parts of Central, India, tradition has fixed twelve[3] as the usual number of artisans in a village. But this is seldom, if ever, found to correspond to the actual number, though twelve may be regarded as a fair mean between the variations in different localities. The origin of the services is probably to be found in the isolated condition of villages when communications were scanty and undeveloped and the individual village was thrown largely on its own resources to supply the needs of daily life. Each of the professions represented in a village has in the majority of cases become crystallized into a caste with its customary duties and monopolies. The original method of remunerating the village servants was *either* by giving them a grant of land free of rent and sometimes free of revenue, *or* by giving them definite shares out of the common heap of grain on the threshing-

[1] This organization of village artisans is not found in Burma or Assam, and is hardly perceptible in Bengal proper.

[2] E.g. *Punjab District Gazetteers*, Jullundur, pp. 211–12; *Bengal District Gazetteers*, Patna, p. 45; *United Provinces District Gazetteers*, Basti, pp. 105–8; *Central Provinces and Berar District Gazetteers*, Raipur, pp. 174–5.

[3] *Burra Bullootee*, Elphinstone, *Report on the Territories Conquered from the Paishwa*, p. 20 Wilks, *Historical Sketches of South India*, Madras, 1869, p. 75 (footnote).

floor or from the individual harvest of every villager, *or* by combining grants of land and of grain—supplemented in each case by various occasional perquisites. All these forms of payment have survived to this day, in varying degrees. But payment by cash is becoming increasingly common; and there has been noticeable, in common with other sides of village life, a growing weakening of customary bonds and assertion of individual rights. Originally, at any rate, the idea must have been that the artisans were public servants of the village,[1] and in return for their grants of land or grain they were required to serve every member of the community on demand. In this respect they seem to afford an interesting parallel to the common innkeeper, the common hogman, the common farrier, and other communal servants of early England.[2]

20. The three principal officers of the village—the Headman, the Accountant, and the Watchman—though still in charge of important administrative duties, have become more the servants of Government than of the village community. The hereditary principle is still largely recognized, but the revenue officers of Government may exercise their discretion in accepting or rejecting a candidate. The importance of the headman in the Non-Landlord villages of Bombay, Madras, and Burma has been noticed before. His specific functions will be described more fully in succeeding chapters. It is sufficient to notice here that in these provinces there is scarcely a department of village life into which his duties do not penetrate, while in the Landlord villages of Upper India he is almost exclusively a revenue official. The accountant's main duties are to maintain the records and keep the accounts connected with land revenue. He may be

[1] From a South Indian inscription of the tenth century A.D. it would appear that each village owned a certain number of looms in common, and the weavers who worked them were maintained out of the village fund. Any other looms would be unauthorized.—*Epigraphia Indica*, Calcutta, vol. iv, p. 138.

[2] *The Common Law*, O. W. Holmes, Jr., Macmillan, 1882, Lecture v.

looked upon, at least in the villages in South India, as the financial and ministerial assistant of the headman, as the village watchman may be regarded as the executive assistant. The watchman everywhere holds an inferior position. He is drawn, as a rule, from the menial castes who live on the outskirts of the village. Some of his duties as general servant to the community are so degrading that the doors of village society are shut against him. The remuneration of all these officers now takes the form, to a large extent, of payment by cash, either by fixed salaries or by a certain percentage of commission on the revenue.[1] The old method of payment by grants of land or in kind has, with a few exceptions,[2] been done away with.

21. The most characteristic feature of the government of a village community was the *panchayat* or village council. The word *panchayat* possibly indicates that the number of those who originally constituted the council was five. But there is no evidence that this number was adhered to with any regularity. The term has almost completely lost its numerical connotation and means only an association of people for doing administrative or judicial work. The learned writer of the last *Punjab Census Report*[3] points out that the number five is one of frequent occurrence in Indian sacred literature. He seems to imply, though he does not say it, that the term *panchayat* was chosen for its sacred associations rather than for any definite numerical indication.[4] And this seems to receive corroboration from current proverbs regarding the

[1] *Imperial Gazetteer of India*, vol. iv, pp. 227, 281.

[2] E.g. village watchmen in Bombay and the Central Provinces are still paid by land or in kind.

[3] Pandit Harikishen Kaul, *Punjab Census*, 1911.

[4] See note by Sir F. Pollock (Maine's *Ancient Law*, 1896, Note P to chap. viii): "We are free to hold as a pious opinion that the Indian village council still known as the Five (*Panchayat*) . . . may go back to the same origin as our own reeve and four men, who flourish in Canada to this day. Robuster faith might be needed to find more than accident in the number of five hearths and five lawful men on Horace's estate."

divine sanction of the *panchayat.* One of the commonest is—"There is God in the *panch.*"[1] There is no doubt, however, that in spite of their great traditional sanctity, *panchayats* have now dropped considerably out of use. At the last census in India, the provincial superintendents were specifically directed to investigate the existence of village *panchayats*; and most of them returned the opinion that practically no trace of them was left.

22. It, however, remains true that there are various local matters which the inhabitants of a village manage among themselves without materially seeking the assistance of outside authorities. The management of private schools, the construction and repair of school buildings, tanks and wells, the distribution of water in lands under irrigation, the settlement of small disputes, the common enjoyment of grazing and woodcutting in forests, the administration of village co-operative credit societies—these are some of the matters in which village communities even now show a perceptible amount of common life and purpose. In face of these, it seems somewhat too facile to say that the old communal institutions of the village have died out altogether. The facts, at any rate, warrant a very careful inquiry.

23. The writers of the *Bombay Census Report* (1911), finding numerous traces of caste or professional *panchayats* but none of the village as a whole, ventured the suggestion that all *panchayats* have been caste *panchayats*, that the myth of the village *panchayat* has probably arisen from the fact that a village is generally, if not invariably, formed by several families of some one caste settling in one spot.[2] The suggestion is rendered plausible by the fact that in the two cases of artificial village communities noted before (Paras.

[1] Compare Russian proverb, "What the *Mir* has settled, is God's own judgment" (Leroy Beaulieu, *The Empire of the Tsars*, App. to Part I, Bk. VIII).

[2] *Bombay Census Report*, 1911, p. 200.

13 and 14), the villages were in each case made up of families belonging to the same caste (Sudras in the *Arthaśāstra* and Brahmans in the South Indian inscription). But over against this must be set certain other evidences which point in a different direction. In the *Manasara Silpasastra* to which Mr. Havell refers, among the different plans for laying out a village is one designed explicitly for the accommodation of a village community composed of different castes.[1] Similarly in the so-called Code of Manu the committees for interpreting the sacred law might be composed of people belonging to any of the first three orders.[2] According to the *Madras Epigraphic Report for* 1912–13, there were village assemblies in South India in the tenth century A.D., which "appear to have consisted of all the residents of a village, including cultivators, professionals, and merchants."[3] In the *Private Diary of Anandaranga Pillay*, who served as agent to Dupleix, the French Governor in South India in the middle of the eighteenth century, there is an entry referring to a village meeting to consider a case of desecrating the village temple "in which people of all castes—from the Brahman to the Pariah—took part."[4]

24. The term *panchayat* might denote either a general meeting of the inhabitants or a select committee chosen from among them. The two forms are very often found side by side in the same community. But on the facts under observation, the suggestion may be made that, as a rule, general meetings of villagers are more in evidence in less developed communities like those of the aboriginal tribes, and select committees in the more highly

[1] *Essay on the Architecture of the Hindus*, Rām Rāz, pp. 44–5. *Ancient and Medieval Architecture of India*, Havell, p. 15.

[2] *Mānava Dharma Śāstra*, ch. xii, pp. 109–13 (Jones & Haughton, Calcutta).

[3] P. 28.

[4] *The Private Diary of Anandaranga Pillay*, J. F. Price, Madras, 1914, vol. i, pp. 332–3.

organized communities. If we take two such aboriginal races as the *Santals* in Bengal and the *Oraons* in Chota Nagpur—both of whom show evidences of a vigorous system of village communities—we find that whenever there is an important matter requiring decision, the headman summons a meeting of all adult males belonging to the village.[1] On the other hand, if we take village communities in settled kingdoms like those pictured in the Code of Manu, or in South Indian inscriptions of the tenth century A.D., we find in each village a small select body or bodies chosen on some recognized principle to whom local administration is practically entrusted. While this broad difference between developed and undeveloped communities may to a large extent be tenable, in the great mass of village communities it would be futile to trace anything approaching to a clear administrative organization. The *panchayat* is often a nebulous thing which appears, in the minds of the villagers, to drift between the idea of a meeting of the whole community and the idea of a more or less select council.

25. Sir Henry Maine, in one of his Lectures, remarked: "India has nothing answering to the assembly of adult males which is so remarkable a feature of the ancient Teutonic groups, except the Council of Village Elders."[2] The general gathering of villagers among such communities as those of the *Santals* and the *Oraons* would perhaps correspond in a rough way to the Teutonic assembly and be an answer to Maine's remark. His explanation of the absence of the assembly of adult males in India is noteworthy. The Indian village community was rarely a community in arms, like the Teutonic; and there was not therefore the same inducement to assign importance to the younger men. All that was required

[1] *Bengal Census Report*, 1911, pp. 472, 474.
[2] *Village Communities in the East and West*, Lecture iv, p. 122.

was civil wisdom, for which they resorted to a close group of village elders. From this point of view it is interesting to observe that among the *Santals* the general meeting of villagers often takes place in connection with the big hunting expeditions undertaken during the hot weather. The convener of the hunt sends word round "notifying the date and place of the hunt and also the place where the people are to spend the night. They reach the spot at sunset after the hunt is over, cook their food, and then take up any matter which may be brought before the people in council assembled."[1]

26. But general meetings of villagers, and sometimes of whole groups of villages, might also be traced, though rarely, among more advanced communities in early times. In one of the reports of the Madras Epigraphic Department, there is an account of some inscriptions relating to the administration of criminal law in South India in the twelfth century A.D. "A certain individual shot a man belonging to his own village by mistake. Thereupon the *governor and the people of the district* to which the village belonged assembled together and decided that the culprit should not die for the offence committed by him through carelessness," but should instead burn a lamp in the temple. In another inscription dealing with a similar matter, the governor is not mentioned, but only the people of the district. "Consequently the people of the district appear to have played a more important part at such trials than even the governor himself."[2] An inscription of about A.D. 1054 sets out the following incident. A village officer demanded taxes from a woman, who declared she was not liable. The former seems to have put her through an ordeal. The woman took poison and died. A meeting of the people from "the four

[1] *Bengal District Gazetteers*, Santal Parganas, pp. 106–12.
[2] *Madras Epigraphy*, *Annual Report*, 1899–1900, p. 11.

quarters, eighteen districts, and the various countries" was held. The man was declared guilty and fined.[1]

27. A good example of a select committee is found in the Code of Manu in the appointment of small boards for interpreting doubtful questions of law. When we bear in mind that law as understood in the Code of Manu covers social and administrative matters besides law proper, a committee of this kind appears to bear a strong resemblance to the ordinary village *panchayat*.[2] It was to consist of from three to ten members, preferably of Brahmans or of men belonging to the three highest castes, of whom in any case there was to be a minimum of three. The chief qualification for membership was proficiency in the sacred writings. The committee, which was probably appointed by the king, was to meet under the direction of a headman. If there was difficulty in getting a sufficient number of men together, the following provision was laid down for guidance: "Even the decision of one priest, if more cannot be assembled, who perfectly knows the principles of the Vedas, must be considered as law of the highest authority; not the opinion of myriads who have no sacred knowledge." [3]

28. For the decision of disputes between two villages or between inhabitants of the same village, rules for the appointment of judicial boards are laid down in some of the early books. The *Arthaśāstra* contains the following: "In all disputes regarding the boundary between any two villages, neighbours or elders of five or ten villages shall investigate the case on the evidence to be furnished from natural or artificial boundary marks." Disputes arising in the same village "shall be decided by the elders of the neighbourhood or of the village. If they are divided in their opinions, decision shall be sought for in such a place as is noted

[1] *Madras Epigraphy, Annual Report*, 1906–7, p. 71.

[2] *Census of India*, 1911, vol. i, p. 395.

[3] *Mānava Dharma Śāstra*, ch. xii, pp. 109–13 (Jones & Haughton).

for a number of pure and respectable people. Or, the disputants may equally divide the disputed holding among themselves. If both of these methods fail, the holding under dispute shall be taken possession of by the king."[1] The *Śukra-nīti* lays down: "Foresters are to be tried with the help of foresters, merchants by merchants, soldiers by soldiers, and in the village (?) by persons who live with both parties."[2]

29. On this subject of disputes regarding boundaries, the Code of Manu has some detailed provisions:—

"If a contest arise between two villages, or landholders, concerning a boundary, let the king or his judge ascertain the limits in the month of Jyaishta,[3] when the landmarks are seen more distinctly.

"Should there be a doubt, even on the inspection of those marks, recourse must be had, for the decision of such a contest, to the declaration of witnesses.

"These witnesses must be examined concerning the landmarks, in the presence of all the townsmen or villagers, or of both the contending parties.

"If there be no witnesses, let four men, who dwell on all the four sides of the two villages, make a decision concerning the boundary, being duly prepared, like the witnesses, in the presence of the king.

"If there be no such neighbours on all sides, nor any men whose ancestors had lived there since the villages were built, nor other inhabitants of towns who can give evidence on the limits, the judge must examine the following men who inhabit the woods:—

"Hunters, fowlers, herdsmen, fishers, diggers for roots, catchers of snakes, gleaners, and other foresters.

"Should the neighbours say anything untrue, when two men dispute about a landmark, the king shall make

[1] *Mysore Review*, July 1908.

[2] *Sacred Books of the Hindus*, vol. xiii (Allahabad, 1914), ch. iv, sec. v, pp. 44–5. The *Sukra-Niti* is a political composition somewhat similar to the *Arthaśāstra* but probably much later.

[3] May–June (Wilson).

each of these witnesses pay the middlemost of the three usual amercements." [1]

30. By far the fullest account of early village committees which we possess is contained in South Indian inscriptions relating to the Tamil kingdoms of the tenth century A.D., recently brought under notice. The most important of these are two inscriptions discovered in a temple in the Uttaramallur village in the Chingleput district.[2] The Chola King Parāntaka I was then reigning over the greater part of the Tamil country. It was during his reign, which probably lasted from A.D. 907 to 947–8 that the events recorded in these inscriptions transpired. There had been gross mismanagement of communal affairs in the village for some time, and it became necessary to interpose the royal authority. The village was a Brahman settlement, perhaps of the kind noticed in paragraph 14. The king at first sent a royal commissioner of the Sudra caste to arrange a settlement. This is the arrangement recorded in the earlier of the two inscriptions. But partly on account of the inexperience of this officer and partly owing to the caste prejudice against him, the settlement did not work, and so the king had to interfere again. This time he sent a Brahman officer, who apparently succeeded with the support of the villagers in framing a satisfactory constitution. The later inscription, which is the fuller of the two, sets forth this new constitution. The differences between the two inscriptions are comparatively matters of detail. It will be sufficient for our purpose to notice the chief features brought out in the second inscription, which is the clearer and fuller of the two.

31. The main fact which we get out of the inscriptions is the existence of several small committees for

[1] *Mānava Dharma Sāstra*, ch. viii, pp. 245–63 (Jones & Haughton).

[2] *Archæological Survey of India*, 1904–5, Calcutta, p. 130. *Madras Epigraphy, Annual Report*, 1898–9, p. 23.

local administration in the same village. The designation of each committee gives some rough indication of its sphere of work. The following is a list of six committees:—

(1) Annual Committee.
(2) Garden Committee.
(3) Tank Committee.
(4) Gold Committee.
(5) Committee of Justice.
(6) A Committee styled *Pancha-Vara*.

There is evidence that the fifth committee, that of Justice, was not perhaps a separate committee but one of the other committees sitting in a different capacity. The term *Pancha-Vara* which occurs in the name of the last committee has not been clearly explained. Two meanings have been suggested: (*a*) that it is a committee for general supervision, and (*b*) that it is entrusted with the collection of a special tax.[1] The second seems more likely, since the first committee which occurs in the inscription without a specific description of its work would more probably have the work of general supervision in its hands. It has been suggested that the village officers were members of the Annual Committee, in which case there would be some likelihood that they must have constituted the premier committee in the village. In an inscription from another district there is mention made of five other committees.[2] It is, therefore, possible that there was no fixed rule on the point, but the needs and opinions of each locality determined the number of its committees.

32. On one point we are still looking for clear light. And that is, whether these committees were subcommittees of a larger assembly or whether they were independent and unco-ordinated committees. The

[1] *Madras Epigraphy*, *Annual Report*, 1912–13, p. 104.
[2] *Ibid.*, 1904–5, p. 49.

former seems more probable. In the two inscriptions under consideration, the casting of lots for electing members to the various committees is to take place before "a full meeting of the great assembly, including young and old." An inscription of King Rajaraja Chola I (A.D. 985–1013) in the Tanjore district mentions forty villages "where the villagers, as a body, seem to have managed their affairs."[1] These cases would suggest the possibility of a larger council in the village, perhaps comprising the whole of the adult community. The wording of what are known as the *Ukkal Inscriptions*, noticed in an earlier Epigraphic Report, has been held to represent these committees rather distinctly as sub-committees of a larger assembly.[2] If this suggestion is true, we have yet to know anything, even tolerably definite, about the constitution of the larger assembly—whether it included all the residents, how often it met, or what its duties were. On this last point we get some glimpse in the fact that every member of the committees was bound to give "an account of his stewardship" immediately before or after the expiry of his term of office. Probably the account was rendered to the general assembly.

33. The mode of election to the committees was as follows: The village with its twelve streets was divided into thirty wards. Every one who lived in these wards wrote a name on a ticket. The tickets were first arranged in separate bundles representing the thirty wards. Each bundle bore the name of the ward to which it belonged. The bundles were then collected and put into a pot and placed before the general body of inhabitants both "young and old" in meeting assembled. All the priests were required to be present. The oldest priest among those present then took the pot, and "looking upwards so as to be seen by all people" called one of the "young boys"

[1] *Archæological Survey of India*, 1904–5, p. 130.
[2] *South Indian Inscriptions*, vol. iii, part i, pp. 1–22, Madras, 1899.

standing close by "who does not know what is inside" to pick out one of the bundles. The tickets in this bundle were then removed to another pot. After it had been well shuffled, the boy took one ticket out of this bundle and handed it to an officer called the *Arbitrator*, who received it "on the palm of his hand with the five fingers open." He read out the name, and it was then shouted out by the priests present in the assembly. Thirty names were thus selected representing each of the wards. Out of these thirty, twelve were appointed to the Annual Committee (1), twelve to the Garden Committee (2), and six to the Tank Committee (3). For the other two committees, Gold and *Pancha-Vara*, (4) and (6) (the Committee of Justice (5) was probably not a separate committee), the whole process was gone through again from the beginning. Of the thirty names thus chosen, eighteen were eliminated. The rest, twelve, were divided equally between the two Committees. The process by which out of the thirty names this elimination and further selection takes place, here as well as in the first three committees, or at least two of them, is denoted in the inscription by the Tamil phrase *Karai-Kātti*. For the present it may be explained, according to the tentative meaning put on it by the late Superintendent of Epigraphy, as an "oral expression of opinion." What this may mean will be indicated later.

34. The chief qualifications for membership in the committees may be summarized thus :—

(1) The person must own more than a quarter *vēli* [1] of tax-paying land.

(2) He must live in a house built on his own site.

(3) He must be below 70 and above 35 years of age.

[1] *Vēli* is about five acres—Winslow.

(4) He must have knowledge of the *Mantras* and the *Brahmanas*. Knowledge of certain specially important sacred writings will make up for a defective property qualification.

(5) He must be conversant with business.

(6) He must be virtuous and his earnings must be honest.

(7) He must not have been on any of the committees for three previous years.

(8) One who has been a member before, but failed to render a proper account, and all his relations, must be excluded.

(9) Those who have been guilty of certain grave sins are also ineligible.

There are references here and there to women members on village committees, and apparently women were under no absolute prohibition.[1]

35. It would be interesting, if materials were available, to form some idea of the procedure followed at a village meeting. But hardly any materials are available, and all that can be attempted is to indicate what it might be. It is perhaps necessary to get rid of the notion that the forms of Western democratic communities, or anything really akin to them, were in operation in the Indian village community. From the days of Lord Metcalfe, the village communities of India have been frequently described as "little republics";[2] and some confusion has undoubtedly resulted by applying to them a term which has come to bear certain concrete political associations. From the facts set out in the early books and inscriptions, it appears that where village committees were not appointed by the king or his officers, as they probably were in the *Arthaśāstra* and in Manu, they were

[1] *Madras Epigraphy*, *Annual Report*, 1909–10, p. 98.

[2] For Metcalfe's famous description of the Indian village community, see Baden-Powell, *Land Systems of British India*, vol. i, p. 170.

appointed by the villagers casting lots. In neither case have we a system of election which aimed at determining the collective will of the community. The will which prevailed in the appointment of village committees, so far as these facts can guide us, was either the Will of the King or the supposed Will of the Supernatural.

36. Nor shall we be safe in assuming that there was anything like a process of division at village meetings with a view to letting the majority decide. That there was ample discussion, loud and eloquent, we may be sure. In one of the Telugu inscriptions eloquence at village meetings is extolled as a special merit.[1] The *Hitopadesa* lays down "eloquence in assembly" as one of the qualities of the "perfect, high-minded" man.[2] But what perhaps happened when a decision was necessary was that in the course of the discussion the opinions of the more influential and wise gradually, and perhaps unconsciously, overbore the rest. The result was a unanimous decision—the product of two things, the assertion of the stronger and the acquiescence of the weaker. A unanimous decision rather than a majority was the thing aimed at, and very often secured. An inscription of the ninth century A.D., discovered in Tinnevelly, lays down as a rule for the conduct of the village assembly that members should, in no case, persistently oppose by saying "nay," "nay," to every proposal brought before the assembly.[3]

37. Sir Herbert Risley once expressed this point with great clearness as follows: "The method by which the *Panchayat* is elected cannot be expressed in terms of European political phraseology. The people get together and they talk, and eventually an opinion emerges from their talk which is the opinion

[1] *Archæological Survey of India*, 1904–5.

[2] *Hitopadesa*, "Acquisition of Friends," sec. 32 (Francis Johnson, 1847). The *Hitopadesa* is an ancient Sanskrit work, classed by Hindu writers as a work on *Nīti* or polity, and designed for the instruction of princes, to prepare them for the duties of their future lives.

[3] *Madras Epigraphy*, *Annual Report*, 1912–13, p. 98.

of all of them. There is no majority, for they are unanimous; there is no minority, for the minority has been talked over and casts in its lot with the majority. The process can only be described as selection by acclamation, in the way the earliest Greek and German popular bodies were selected, the oldest mode of election in the world." [1] It may be suggested here that it is this process of selection which is possibly referred to in the Uttaramallur inscription by the Tamil word *Karai-Kātti*, if the tentative meaning, "oral expression of opinion," holds good (para. 33). In the first instance, as we saw, thirty names were chosen by casting lots; and then for allotting them to the different committees, what took place was perhaps what Sir Herbert Risley has called "selection by acclamation." The suggestion is at least plausible. Some support will be gained for the point by considering the provision in the *Arthaśāstra* on settlement of village disputes. According to the rendering furnished by a distinguished Mysore scholar,[2] if the elders are divided in their opinion, a decision shall be sought for at the hands of "pure and respectable" people in another village, or the property is divided between the disputants, or it goes to the king (para. 28). There is no reference here to decision by a majority. If there was a division of opinion, the thing to do, apparently, was not to take the opinion of the majority but to have the matter settled by certain other means specified in the rule.[3]

[1] Speech, Bengal Legislative Council, July 23, 1892. There is an interesting note on the point in Maitland's *Township and Borough* (pp. 34-5), "one of the great books that remain to be written is The History of the Majority . . . In the earlier Middle Ages it is unanimity that is wanted. . . . A shout is the test, and in form it is the primary test to-day in the House of Commons. But the few should not go on shouting when they know that they are few. If they do, measures can be taken to make them hold their peace. In the end the assembly has but one voice, one audible voice; it is unanimous."

[2] Professor Sama Sastry.

[3] A different rendering of this passage was given by a learned writer from Bengal in the *Modern Review* (Calcutta) June 1913 (footnote to p. 666), by which in case of a difference of opinion, the question was to be settled by "an honest majority." One ventures to think that this is based on a slight misconception.

38. On the connection, if any, which existed between the local government of the village community and the central government of the king, there is before us no satisfactory evidence. It is fairly clear that during the period of Muhammadan rule, the village communities were left more or less to their own resources; and practically no connection was maintained with the king's government, except the due payment of the taxes. So long as these were paid regularly, there was no inducement for a government, almost entirely fiscal like that of the Mughals, to interfere in matters of local administration. "This separation has stamped itself in the language of the people. The terms for the village and its internal life are almost everywhere taken from the vernacular Indian speech; but beyond the village stretched the Persian *Zila* or district, and beyond the *Zila* the Persian *Sūbah* or province, whose capital formed the residence of the remote government or Persian *Sirkar*." [1]

39. During the Hindu period, however, there is evidence that the isolation of the village was, at any rate, not quite so pronounced as in Muhammadan times. And in the little glimpses which we are allowed into some of the Hindu kingdoms of the past, the impression arises that the village was regarded in a real sense as part of the realm, and entitled to the protection and constant care of the king. There were officers of the king, of varying degrees of authority, through whom the king maintained watch over the villages. But it does not appear that, as a rule, there was "anything of the nature of a political institution between the village and the Central Government," [2] nor any administrative unit between the village and the kingdom which had a recognized place in the consciousness of the people. In explaining the law of sacrifice, the *Hitopadesa* says: "A man should leave

[1] Sir W. W. Hunter, speech in the Imperial Legislative Council, September 12, 1883.
[2] *Ibid.*

a single person for the sake of a family; for the sake of a village, he should abandon a family; a village he should renounce for the sake of a country; and the whole world for the sake of his soul." [1]

40. In the Code of Manu, the connection of the king with the village is of a very direct kind, the headman himself being appointed by him.[2] The *Arthas'āstra* describes a vast arrangement of espionage by which the king might be kept in touch with the affairs of the village.[3] The *S'ukra-Nīti* requires the king to inspect the villages personally every year. He "must know which subjects have been pleased and which oppressed by the staff of officers and deliberate upon the matters brought forward by the people." [4] The South Indian inscriptions mention various facts to show the more or less intimate connection which existed between the village community and the king. A village assembly misappropriated some money which had been ear-marked for the temple. The temple authorities thereupon complained to the king. The king sent for both the parties, and after due inquiry satisfied himself of the guilt of the assembly. They were fined and the money was restored to the temple.[5] An inscription of about A.D. 1291 speaks of a village assembly which made a report to the king about the misconduct of a Brahman member who brought a "widow from a foreign country" and lived with her. The king's decision is not given.[6] In another inscription the same village assembly wishing to pay their respects to the king alienated some land to raise money for the cost of the journey.[7] An inscription of A.D. 1303 refers to a successful appeal made to the king by a village assembly against a man

[1] *Hitopadesa*, "Acquisition of Friends," sec. 158 (Francis Johnson).
[2] *Mānava Dharma Sāstra*, ch. viii, sec. 115 (Jones & Haughton).
[3] *Mysore Review*, February 1908.
[4] *Sacred Books of the Hindus*, vol. xiii (Allahabad, 1914), ch. i, secs. 751–2.
[5] *Madras Epigraphy, Annual Report*, 1906–7, p. 71.
[6] *Ibid.*, 1908–9, p. 83.
[7] *Ibid.*, p. 84.

who intruded into the village and succeeded in intimidating the assembly and confining the members in the temple.[1] Then there is a case of a village appropriating some of its revenues towards securing the friendship of the king's agents.[2] And another raising money for the performance of public prayers on behalf of a sick member of the royal family.[3] Treason against the king was severely dealt with in the villages. In A.D. 1230 we read of a village where lands belonging to certain persons who were the declared enemies (*drohin*) of the State were sold by public auction, the price bring fixed by eight officers of the king.[4] In another case the king is mentioned as appointing a new headman in a village for the specific purpose of dealing with certain persons who were traitors to the king (*Raja-drohin*).[5] The usual practice for the king when he thought interference necessary and possible was to send a special commissioner to the village to act in his name. The arrangements recorded in the Uttaramallur inscriptions were the work of such commissioners. In other inscriptions we read of the clerk of the village assembly writing down its proceedings while "the magistrate (i.e. the royal officer) was walking about."[6]

41. When Sir Henry Maine said that "in the almost inconceivable case of disobedience to the award of the village council, the sole punishment or the sole certain punishment would appear to be universal disapprobation,"[7] he made what, to a large extent, appears to be a true statement. But in the light of such facts as those set out above, showing how the king interfered, and was asked to interfere, in various village matters, it seems reasonable to infer that in kingdoms which had reached a certain degree of organization, the ultimate

[1] *Madras Epigraphy, Annual Report*, 1908–9, p. 83.
[2] *Ibid.*, 1912–13, p. 114.
[3] *Ibid.*, 1899–1900, p. 20.
[4] *Ibid.*, 1910–11, p. 75.
[5] *Ibid.*, 1912–13, p. 110.
[6] *South Indian Inscriptions*, vol. iii, part ii, p. 173.
[7] *Village Communities in the East and West*, Lecture iii, pp. 68–9.

sanction was not merely the disapprobation of the community but punishment by the king. According to the *Arthas'āstra*, defamation of one's village is an offence punishable with a fine.[1] It may be inferred, therefore, that disobedience to an award of the village council would be an equal, if not a greater, offence, and punishable by the king. In one of the South Indian inscriptions, of about A.D. 1230, a village assembly decided that any one who did anything against the interests of the village or the temple "should suffer as the *grama-drohins* (injurers of the village) do."[2] The use of the expression "should suffer as the *grama-drohins* do" would show that to injure the interests of the village was a recognized form of offence in the kingdom, corresponding to the offence of *Raja-droha*, or injuring the interests of the king. A similar term, *Grama-Kantaka*,[3] is used in the Uttaramallur inscription. The provision that such men are to be debarred from certain temple ceremonies points to a religious sanction in addition to the other sanctions.

42. A good picture of a sitting of a present-day village *panchayat* in one of the Tamil districts is contained in a sketch of South Indian life published in Madras some time ago, *Thillai Govindan*.[4] The business before the meeting was to consider the misconduct of the village schoolmaster in inflicting an exceptionally severe form of punishment on one of the boys (who is the hero of the story). The meeting was held in the house of the boy's grandfather, one of the most respected men in the village. "The parliament consisted of about twenty-five members, of whom eighteen were Brahmans and the rest *Sudras*. It was very slow in coming together,

[1] *Mysore Review*, January 1909.

[2] *Madras Epigraphy*, *Annual Report*, 1910–11, p. 75.

[3] Village pest.

[4] *Madras*, ch. v. The author is an Indian officer in the Madras Excise Department, and is well known in South India as a careful observer of Indian social life and a thoughtful and original writer.

and many a member had to be specially sent for; so that, though its sitting was announced for 3 p.m., it was nearing 5 when about twenty members had gathered. . . . The Brahman members sat on the raised [platform] and the others on the verandah below —they were all chewing [betel leaves] at our expense, and tobacco snuff was also handed round freely. My grandfather opened the proceedings by saying that they had met to punish the conduct of the schoolmaster who had treated me cruelly, that the punishment of a fine of one rupee once before inflicted on him seemed to have had no effect, and that though he had decided not to send me to his school any longer . . . it was necessary, in the interests of the other pupils, to guard against such occurrences in the future; and he recommended the dismissal of Sundaram Iyer (the schoolmaster). This speech was preceded by a preamble dwelling on the speaker's absolute indifference to mundane affairs, and his entire disinterestedness in what he was going to utter. . . . On hearing this, the schoolmaster, who was also present, expressed his great remorse at what had happened, promised most solemnly to behave better in future, dwelt on his long service of nearly thirty years, and the fact that several of his present judges were once his pupils . . . stating in conclusion that if they dismissed him in his old age, he and his family would have to starve and die at the doors of the members. A Sudra member insisted on the teacher's dismissal, and informed the assembly that a more learned and capable teacher was available for service in the next village. Another member spoke of the foolishness of sparing the rod with children, and heroically boasted that he had suffered the punishment (i.e. of the form complained of) thrice during his schooldays. 'And all to no purpose,' muttered another, and those around him laughed gaily. In the end the schoolmaster was fined five rupees and advised to treat his boys better in future. The parliament having assembled and being ready for business, a case of house-breaking and theft was brought to its notice. This had occurred a month ago in a Brahman's house, and had been immediately reported to the police-station. The police then inquired into the matter, and finding the complainant unwilling to help them as they proposed, and seeing no chance of detection, had 'referred' the case as false. . . . This case was now taken up, and as the members were aware of the truth of the theft, the parliament called on the four *Marava* headmen [1] of the village to make good the lost property, which was valued at nearly four hundred rupees. The headmen pleaded that the matter had in the first instance been reported to the police instead of to them, that they had thereby suffered some trouble and loss of money, that the crime was committed by the members of a gang from a distant village, and that in these circumstances they could not be held liable for the property. Their objections were partly recognized, and the complainant was fined twenty rupees for seeking police help without the permission of the village parliament, the fine to be credited to the village parliament. Then the value of the jewels lost was discussed at length, and was finally reduced to three hundred rupees. The headmen were required to make good this amount within a week, and they agreed to do so. It was nearly dark by this time, and the assembly then broke up gradually." [2]

43. The village community has now lost much of its internal cohesion. Many of the administrative duties which in more leisurely and less exacting days were left to be done by the village commuity have

[1] Headmen of criminal tribes engaged by the villagers privately for police purposes.

[2] There is a rather striking resemblance between this description and that of a village meeting in Russia given in Wallace's *Russia*, ch. viii (1912).

had necessarily to be taken up into the hands of the Central Government and its subordinate agencies. The progress of education and the rising spirit of individualism are helping this process from within. Nevertheless, as an administrative organ of great potential usefulness for the rural population the village community is by no means dead. In the words of the Royal Commissioners on Decentralization in India, "the foundation of any stable edifice which shall associate the people with the administration must be the village as being an area of much greater antiquity than (the new administrative creations) and one in which people are known to one another and have interests which converge on well-recognized objects. . . ."[1] Two great movements in India in recent years lend a new significance to the question—the growth of co-operative credit societies and the extension of primary education. When the load of indebtedness has been lifted off his shoulders and his mind awakened to the meaning of the things around him, we may well hope that the Indian villager may develop a new desire to make his personality, however feeble and broken, enter in some positive way into the government of his little world. Even amid the sound of war and the birth-throes of a new world, there is no higher call in India to the men of our generation than to see this process go forward.

[1] Parliamentary Paper, 1909 (Cd. 4360), pp. 238–9.

CHAPTER II

EDUCATION

1. THE history of village education in India goes back perhaps to the beginnings of the village community. The schoolmaster had a definite place assigned to him in the village economy, in the same manner as the headman, the accountant, the watchman, and the artisans. He was an officer of the village community, paid either by rent-free lands or by assignments of grain out of the village harvest. In all likelihood, the earliest schoolmaster was the Brahman priest of the village who offered worship to the village deity on behalf of the different classes of people who lived in the village. From this function discharged by the priest followed his subsidiary function of imparting instruction to those castes who were either of the "twice born" (the superior castes), or were in any way connected with the "twice born" and felt the obligation of acquiring letters. The earliest injunctions bearing on the duties of priests laid upon them the obligation not merely of ministering to religion, but of imparting instruction in the rudiments of knowledge. The lands which supported the priestly schoolmaster were the lands set apart for the village idol, and this income was usually supplemented by free-will offerings from the scholars and their parents.[1]

2. The outstanding characteristics of the schools of

[1] The first four paragraphs of this chapter are practically based upon the *Bengal Report of the Indian Education Commission* (1882–3).

the Hindu village community were: (1) that they were democratic, and (2) that they were more secular than spiritual in their instruction and their general character. The first of these characteristics was apparently a result of the process of absorption with the indigenous population which followed the first stages of the Aryan conquest. The caste system, we read, was extended so as to include non-Aryans, and their deities were accorded places in the Hindu pantheon. It was a characteristic which was shared by the Muhammadan schools which sprang up throughout the country in the Middle Ages, and subsequently by the religious schools started by the Sikhs in the Punjab. Nevertheless, when we speak of the democratic character of these early Hindu schools, it is to be understood that they were democratic only in this sense, that they were open not merely to the priestly caste but to all the four superior castes alike. There was never any question of admitting into the schools those who lay outside the regular caste system whose touch would have meant pollution, nor to the great aboriginal populations of the country. Throughout the long history of indigenous education in India, it is impossible to find any indications that these classes ever came within the range of the vast system of public schools which existed in the country from ancient times.

3. The second characteristic of the schools of the village community, namely, that they were secular, is surprising when we consider that religion has entered so largely at all times into the life of the people and that the earliest instrument of education was the village priest. The reason for this is probably to be found in the circumstance that the teaching of the *Sāstras* was forbidden to all but the priestly class, and that from the earliest times the village schools were meant for the instruction of all the superior castes without distinction. It is likely that prayers might

have been offered in the course of the day's work, and that moral precepts were strengthened by the teaching of sacred legends, but anything in the nature of direct religious instruction was unknown. The principal ingredients of the village curriculum were reading, writing, and arithmetic in the vernacular, with occasionally a dose of Sanskrit grammar and poetry. The secular character of the schools was strengthened by the advent of Buddhism. The immense influence which was exercised on Hinduism by the new faith led to a certain disintegration of the position of the Brahman priest, which necessarily reacted on the character of the schools in which he taught. "It is to the Buddhistic time, in all probability, that we must trace the beginnings of that change under which the village schoolmaster is not found to be invariably the village priest and Brahman, as he certainly was in early Hindu times."[1]

4. The effect of the Muhammadan invasions upon the national educational system was twofold. In the first place, they led to a widespread disorganization of the indigenous schools by interfering with the customary rights of the village community and by the exactions of new landlords who were ignorant of their immemorial privileges. The introduction of Persian as the new official language of the country was not also without its effect. The ancient institutions of learning which prized the study of Sanskrit and the vernaculars grew less popular, and only the lower classes who were content with the bare elements of letters were found to resort to them. In the second place, the growth of a large Muhammadan community in various parts of the country led to the institution of Muhammadan schools in villages where they predominated. It is probable that these Muhammadan schools, *Maktabs* as they are called, were started

[1] *Indian Education Commission* (1882–3), *Bengal Report*, para. 6.

in imitation[1] of the ancient Hindu schools. They differed from the latter in the insistence they laid upon the religious character of their instruction, but in the position of the schoolmaster, the methods of teaching, and the financial arrangements by which they were maintained, the two systems bore a striking resemblance to each other.

5. The political unsettlement which attended the decline of Muhammadan rule in India and preceded the establishment of the British Empire witnessed a gradual decadence of the village community as an effective form of local polity. The causes which led to this decadence belong to a wider subject than can be covered in this study, but it is obvious that when the British took possession of the country in the different provinces they found that, though in most parts of the country except Western and Central India, there existed a widespread system of national education, so far as they could trace, the position of the schoolmaster had in many cases changed from that of a village servant with a defined position in the community into that of a casual worker—honoured in the village by reason of his sacred calling but not sufficiently identified with the village to hold his ancient place on the village staff. This statement is true in the main, but nevertheless there were various traces left which pointed to the original connection of the schoolmaster with the village economy. The Court of Directors of the East India Company were anxious from the first to utilize whatever had been left of the ancient system and to incorporate it into their own scheme of education. A dispatch issued by them to the local government, which bears the date June 3, 1814, has the following reference to the

[1] This suggestion, which occurs in the *Report of the Indian Education Commission* (1882–3), *Bengal*, is open to question. Baron Haxthausen noticed Muhammadan village schools in parts of Russia (*The Russian Empire*, Haxthausen translated by R. Fairie, Chapman & Hall, 1856, vol. i, ch. x). See also Hughes' *Dictionary of Islam*, p. 107.

village community and the schools connected with it. "This venerable and benevolent institution of the Hindus is represented to have withstood the shock of revolutions, and to its operation is ascribed the general intelligence of the natives as scribes and accountants. We are so strongly persuaded of its great utility that we are desirous you should take early measures to inform yourselves of its present state and that you will report to us the result of your inquiries, affording in the meantime the protection of government to the village teachers in all their just rights and immunities, and marking, by some favourable distinction, any individual amongst them who may be recommended by superior merit or acquirements; for humble as their situation may appear, if judged by a comparison with any corresponding character in this country, we understand those village teachers are held in great veneration throughout India."[1]

6. Though attempts had been made earlier in the century in Madras and Bombay to make a preliminary survey of indigenous schools, it was in Bengal that the first systematic attempt was undertaken by the British Government. The Rev. W. Adam, who was chosen by Lord William Bentinck to report on the vernacular schools of Bengal, presented his reports[2] during the years 1835–8, and they still remain among the most valuable records we have regarding indigenous private schools in India. The information has since been supplemented by similar reports from other provinces, by the labours of the Indian Education Commission of 1882–3, presided over by Sir William Hunter, and by the more recent annual and quinquennial reports of the Education Department of India. But before we proceed to describe the main features of indigenous schools, it is necessary to

[1] *Education in British India.* A. Howell, Calcutta, 1872, p. 6.

[2] *Adam's Reports on Vernacular Education in Bengal and Behar.* J. Long, Calcutta, 1868.

describe in outline the present system of village education as a whole in order to bring out more clearly the place of indigenous schools in that system. For, though in some provinces indigenous schools are still responsible for a large share of village education, they are by no means the only agencies of rural education, nor are they often the most important. It will also be necessary, before finishing our survey of indigenous schools, to consider in what respects these schools may be said to come within a purview of village local government.

7. Rural instruction in India is in the hands of either public or private agencies, the latter still constituting the more numerous type. Public agencies in charge of rural education are mostly District Boards, which are the local authorities constituted for each district under the Local Self-Government Scheme of Lord Ripon. Occasionally the educational duties of a District Board are found delegated to a Taluka Board, which is the corresponding local authority for a sub-division of a district. The Provincial Government is seldom in direct charge of primary schools, except in areas where there are no local boards such as the Agency Tracts of the Madras Presidency. The Government, however, retain their control over Board primary schools, partly by rules framed for the guidance of local boards and partly through the inspecting agency of the Education Department.

8. Private schools fall into two classes—those which are aided out of public funds and those which are unaided. A considerable proportion of the aided schools are under the management of foreign missionary and other philanthropic societies, the rest, including the unaided schools, being either indigenous schools or "venture" schools. Indigenous and "venture" schools are found in practice so largely to merge into each other that it is hazardous to attempt a sharp distinction between them, but, broadly speak-

ing, indigenous schools may be said to be the descendants of the old village community schools which, though considerably disorganized and fast disappearing, are still, wherever they are found, in a very intimate way associated with the internal life of the village. "Venture" schools are recent growths. They are started in most cases as business enterprises or in response to a demand by the wealthy inhabitants of a village, by men who merely wish to make a competence out of them. The teachers of indigenous schools come of the ancient hereditary class of *gurus*, but "venture" schools are the products of "uncertificated" teachers whose failure to pass the qualifying examinations laid down by the Education Department debars them from employment in any schools of recognized standing. We are more directly concerned here with the former class of schools, but it may be observed that the distinction between the two classes is fast tending to vanish, the operation of the rules regarding grants in aid and the transformation of the old village life resulting in a gradual assimilation of the two classes of schools towards each other.

9. The following statistics relating to the year 1912–13 of the three oldest provinces will throw some light on the relative numbers of the different classes of schools. In Madras the total number of public elementary schools was 25,211 and of aided elementary schools 14,463. Of the latter about a fifth are under the management of missionary societies. The number of *pial* schools, i.e. unaided indigenous schools, stood at about 4,000 in 1906–7, but must have been reduced considerably in recent years. In Bombay the total number of primary schools was 13,368, of which the number of private aided schools was 2,394 and of private unaided schools 200. The aggregate number of primary schools in Bengal was 36,334, of which 35,899 were private schools—27,474 aided and the rest unaided.

10. The indigenous elementary schools which have

survived in India reveal a striking uniformity as between the different provinces in their constitution and their methods of management and instruction. The variety of customs and characteristics which have prevailed in different parts of the country has apparently had but little effect on the system of education. A *pial* school in Madras is almost identical in character with a *pathsala* in Bengal—and between a *Muktab* in the Punjab and a *Mulla* school in Sind there is hardly any difference. The indigenous schools of India, leaving aside Burma for the present, were started by one or other of these three communities—the Hindu, the Muhammadan, and the Sikh. Except in one particular, namely, that the Muhammadan *Muktab* and *Mulla* school and the Sikh *Gurumukhi* have always made it their main purpose to impart spiritual instruction, while the Hindu *pathsala* has steadily aimed at a secular education, the differences between the three systems of schools are quite inappreciable. Burma in many respects lies outside of India, and its Buddhist monastic schools, the *Pongyi-Kyaungs*, possess characteristics which are peculiar to Burma and require separate notice.

11. The position of the schoolmaster in an indigenous village school is at best a precarious one. His remuneration is made up very largely of presents in cash or kind, supplemented in some cases by fees from his pupils and sometimes by definite assignments from the village harvest. Whether we take the old indigenous school or the new "venture" school, the teacher is himself largely responsible for the management; and whenever, as often happens, the sources of his remuneration fail, he has no choice open to him but to close the school or remove it to some other village where he has a better prospect of steady remuneration. The tradition of gratuitous instruction is still so strong in the country that the payment of fees in a village school is regarded with somewhat

unconcealed prejudice. This probably accounts for the large share taken by occasional presents in the composition of a teacher's income, it being supposed to be a less flagrant violation of the national instinct against paid instruction. Even in cases where schools receiving grants in aid from Government have shown in their periodic returns the rates of fee supposed to be levied by them, it is common knowledge that these so-called fees are more or less hypothetical and that the teacher looks mainly to his perquisites for his maintenance. Whenever a private school is newly started in a village, it is generally in answer to the demand of a few wealthy men in the village who guarantee a living to the teacher, which he supplements by taking in scholars from the poorer families and levying a nominal fee on them. But no teacher would ever feel it safe to rely on these fees or consider it respectable to enforce their collection with due regularity. It was noted by Mr. Adam in 1838 that in each of the Bengal districts a greater or less number of the teachers bestowed their instruction gratuitously, and even teachers who were paid instructed many scholars who paid nothing.[1] The Director of Public Instruction of the United Provinces in his report for 1903-4 makes the following remark: "My own observation leads me to the conclusion that fees are often not levied in aided schools. Managers frequently start these schools to educate their own sons and others in whom they are interested, and they may contribute to the support of the teachers, but there may be no such thing as a fee payable for each scholar, and no payment in money or kind may be made for most of the boys."[2]

12. Besides presents, fees, and contributions, schools which have been recognized by the Government as

[1] *Report*, p. 177.

[2] *United Provinces Annual Report on Education*, 1903-4, p. 27. It will be remembered that the Positivists made it one of their tenets that all education should be given by the teacher gratuitously.

deserving of public support are allowed grants in aid which are estimated in accordance "with the amount of private resources, the qualifications of the teachers, the extent to which the prescribed curriculum is followed, attendance, the numbers in different classes and general efficiency."[1] The grant is paid sometimes by the Provincial Government, sometimes by the District Board, and sometimes by both. The authority by whom the funds are supplied, whether the Provincial Government or the Local Board, has the right of determining the conditions under which grants are allotted and of framing rules for their distribution.

13. The comparative poverty of indigenous schools renders it impossible for the schoolmaster to provide assistance for himself by the appointment of additional teachers. Except in rare cases, an indigenous school has but a single master, and the difficulty of instruction in a growing school is overcome by the system of pupil teachers. The "monitorial system," which made such striking progress in England in the early part of the nineteenth century, received its inspiration, in all likelihood, from the village schools of South India. Dr. Andrew Bell, whose name is associated with the "monitorial system" in England, known as the Bell and Lancaster System, was an Army chaplain in India, and from 1789 to 1796 held the position of Superintendent of the Male Orphan Asylum in Madras. It was in the course of his residence here that his attention was directed to the system of pupil teachers that obtained in the Madras *pial* schools, and which in essence was also the system in the Bengal *pathsalas*.[2]

14. An analysis of the various forms of perquisites paid to a teacher will throw some interesting light on the connection that survives between the village schoolmaster and the village community. The first

[1] *Sixth Quinquennial Report on Education in India* (1907–12), vol. i, p. 119.

[2] Baron Haxthausen noticed the system of mutual instruction in schools in Tatar villages in Russia. Vol. i, ch. x.

thing we note is that the schoolmaster is still regarded as so much a part of the life of the village that, whether he belongs to the old hereditary class or is only his modern equivalent, the "uncertificated" adventurer, at most festivals celebrated in the village, a share of the good things collected for the occasion is set apart for his use. The following account, taken from the evidence of an Inspector of Schools given before the Education Commission (1882–3),[1] relates to a village school in the Salem District of the Madras Presidency. "Every Saturday each boy brings him (the teacher) a little quantity of linseed oil and fuel. On the thirteenth day of the new and full moon boys are required to bring two pice to be given to the teacher. . . . On marriage and harvest days the village teacher is never forgotten, and he gets his share; in fact, he is treated as one belonging to the household of each family, and he shares the common interest of all. During the *Mahanavami*[2] feast, the pupils are trained to dance in a particular fashion, and their performance is exhibited before their parents. The master's income from this source varies according to the size of the village and the circumstances of the residents. . . ." The order of payment in a village school in Tinnevelly was thus described by another witness.[3] "On the third day prior to *Amavasi*,[4] betel-nut is received twice a month. The day previous to *Amavasi* is considered a half-holiday, when each pupil gives two pice or a half measure of paddy. . . . A festival is held in September, when about 20 or 30 rupees is raised from the parents and relatives of the pupils, and another festival in August, when each pupil gives four pice or one anna." The Visitor-General of Schools in the North-West Provinces (the present United Provinces), in his report of 1851 mentioned that in the district he visited:

[1] Dr. John Bradshaw.

[2] Last day of the period dedicated to the worship of the goddess *Durga*.

[3] Rev. V. W. H. Harcourt.

[4] Day of new moon.

"On the *Ekadasi* or 11th of both the light and dark half of every lunar month, each scholar pays in from one *adhela*[1] to two pice. On the several festivals the teacher receives presents of money as well as of clothes and sweetmeats." And in his report for 1901–2, the Director of Public Instruction in Bengal, speaking of perquisites, says, "In rural tracts the monthly fee is always supplemented by *siddhas* or presents in rice, vegetables, oil, pulse, etc., once or twice a month, besides customary gifts on the occasion of a marriage or ceremonies." In Chota Nagpur, "on the occasion of marriage or festivals in the village, the *guru* must have his suit of clothing accompanied also by monthly presents."[2]

15. There is little doubt that the immemorial custom of paying the servants of the village community by assignments out of the periodic harvest still prevails with regard to the schoolmaster in certain parts of the country. Mr. H. S. Reid, in his *Report on Indigenous Education in the North-West Provinces in* 1851, noted that "in villages, when the harvest is cut and deposited in granaries, the schoolmaster comes in for a share varying from two and a half to ten *sers*."[3] The same custom was found to exist in Sind in 1856 among the indigenous Muhammadan schools, where the schoolmaster, especially if he happened to be the village *mulla* (priest), was presented with an allowance of grain each season at harvest.[4] It was common to find in the reports of educational officers in Sind at the time that the master's remuneration was "a pittance of grain each harvest," or "daily food and a small present of grain at harvest." The *Fourth Quinquennial Review of Education* (1897–1902) contains an interesting account by a divisional Inspector of Schools in Bengal of a typical school in a prosperous agricultural

[1] Half a pice.

[2] *Quinquennial Report on Education in Bengal*, 1907–12, para. 244.

[3] Para. 54. A *ser* is generally something over 2 lb. avoirdupois in Bengal.

[4] *Report on Education in Sind*, 1856.

village. "In favourable years, when the cultivation is over, the well-to-do of the villagers select a *guru* of their own caste. These *gurus* teach their children from August to February, live in their house, and are allowed to take their children as their pupils, *on their agreeing to give them a fixed quantity of paddy when the harvest is gathered in*."[1] A well-informed and experienced leader of public opinion in Madras,[2] giving evidence before the Education Commission of 1882–3, said he thought in some parts of the province the *panchangi* or *vadyar* (schoolmaster) was even then paid by grain fees, and argued that it was possible to restore to the village schoolmaster his original position in the community corresponding to the position of the village carpenter, blacksmith, etc. And another Indian witness from the same province,[3] speaking of the remuneration of the teacher, said he had often to wait till the harvest season to get his payment of grain.

16. In some provinces it is not uncommon to find the inhabitants of the village, or at any rate the well-to-do among them, uniting to raise a common fund for the maintenance of the schoolmaster. A typical case was described by Mr. Adam in his Report of 1836 of a school at Dharail, in the Rajshahi District in Bengal, where the leading families of the village contributed in common to the upkeep of a school. Each of them paid a fixed subscription towards the maintenance of the teacher besides permitting him the use of certain outer apartments in their houses. The teacher was at liberty to add to his income by receiving other scholars in the village and receiving fees or presents from them.[4] He also mentions a Muhammadan village in the Hoogly District where "it is said to have been the practice of the Mussalman land proprietors to entertain teachers at their own private cost for the benefit of the children of the poor in the neighbourhood."[5]

[1] P. 174.
[2] The Hon. P. Chentsal Rao, C.I.E.
[3] V. Krishnamachary, Curator of Books.
[4] P. 95.
[5] *Report*, p. 40.

The *Bombay Report of the Education Commission* (1882–3) mentions that in some villages in Bombay, in lieu of fees, the schoolmaster received "a fixed annual income from the villagers, or if a Muhammadan from the Mosque funds." [1] In regard to Sind it was found, in 1856, that in many schools which were set down as free the richer zemindars really subscribed for the maintenance of the teacher.[2]

17. A further relic of the time-honoured connection between the schoolmaster and the village community is to be found in the facility afforded by the villagers in various places for the accommodation of the school in the public buildings which are the common property of the village. Wherever a District Board school does not exist, or the inhabitants are not sufficiently well-to-do or enterprising to build a school for themselves, it is usual, where a school does at all exist, to find it housed in the *chavadi* (meeting-house) or the *dharmsala* (rest-house), or the temple or mosque. In his Report on the schools in the Rajshahi District in Bengal, Mr. Adam pointed out that there were no school-houses built for, and exclusively appropriated to, these schools. "Some meet in the *Chandi Mandap*, which is of the nature of a chapel belonging to some one of the principal families in the village and in which, besides the performance of religious worship on occasion of the great annual festivals, strangers also are sometimes lodged and entertained, and business transacted; others in the *Baithakkhana*, an open hut principally intended as a place of recreation and of concourse for the consideration of any matters relating to the general interests of the village." [3] In Assam the school is not seldom found housed in the village meeting-house, and in parts of Eastern Bengal it is generally held in some outhouse belonging to some village headman.[4] "In Orissa, a lower primary school is not infre-

[1] P. 69. [2] *Report on Education in Sind*, 1856. [3] *Report*, p. 96.
[4] *Eastern Bengal and Assam, Annual Report on Education*, 1905–6, p. 19.

quently held in the village *Bhagabatghar*, a house belonging to the Hindu community of the village and used for the recitation of the Hindu *Puranas*. . . . And in the Burdwan division of Bengal, village *atchalas*, which are practically the Bengali equivalents of the Orissa *Bhagabatghars*, are used for the same purpose.[1] The *Gurumukhi* schools of the Punjab are often held in *dharmsalas*; and whenever a "venture" school is started in any village it is under the roof of the *dharmsala* or mosque that it finds its first accommodation.[2] The *Bombay Quinquennial Report on Education* (1907–12) mentions an interesting case of a village near Poona where the inhabitants were eager to offer the use of the *dharmsala* for the accommodation of a village school and to use the village temple as a *dharmsala* instead. As the Local Taluka Board had a share in the financing of the *dharmsala*, they were entitled to exercise a right of veto in regard to the disposal of it, which, in this case, they exercised against the expressed desire of the villagers. The report goes on to say, "Whenever portions of *chavadis* or *dharmsalas* are given for school use, the people arrange for the accommodation of visitors and travellers elsewhere." In Madras during recent years there has been a perceptible decline in the use of the temples and *chavadis* for the accommodation of schools,[3] the improved resources and enterprise of villagers enabling them to rent or build separate houses for their schools.

18. That there is still an appreciable amount of communal feeling left in villages which impels them on occasions of public necessity to carry out schemes of co-operative improvement is shown by the frequent references in recent educational reports to the interest of villagers in subscribing towards the building of

[1] *Quinquennial Report on Education in Bengal*, 1902–7, p. 58.
[2] *Quinquennial Report on Education in the Punjab*, 1907–12, p. 28.
[3] *Quinquennial Report on Education in Madras*, 1902–7, para. 77.

village school-houses. In places where the material resources of villagers have improved in recent years, they are beginning to awaken to the insufficiency of the old village buildings for the purposes of a school. And partly on their own initiative and partly at the suggestion of Government educational officers, buildings are erected more frequently than before by means of voluntary assessment in cash or in kind. In Madras, where in 1907 the Director of Public Instruction noted a decrease of 25 per cent. in the number of schools housed in *chavadis*, etc., it was stated in the Report: "In several cases the assistance of the villagers was enlisted in the building operations. Some villages provided sites, others materials, labour, or money."[1] Of the rural schools in the Central Provinces, Mr. H. Sharp says in his *Occasional Reports*, i: "The school building is sometimes the gift of the *malguzar* (the landlord), or is erected wholly or partially by subscription among the villagers." In the case of Board schools, the work of building is often entrusted to the village school committee, consisting of the village elders. "Not only is the work honestly and economically performed, but the villagers will exceed the original cost by something out of their own pocket or effect a saving by supplying timber, etc., gratis."[2] In Assam, if there is a house for the village school, it is commonly supposed to be kept in repair by the villagers and the *gurus*.[3]

19. The position of the schoolmaster is strengthened by some subsidiary offices which he has held, and still holds, by customary right and which make him an almost indispensable factor in the life of the village community. In Malabar, in the Madras Presidency, he is frequently the village astrologer (*panikkar*), and the dignity of his position has ever been upheld by a judi-

[1] *Quinquennial Report on Education in Madras*, 1902–7, para. 77.
[2] *Calcutta*, 1904, p. 49.
[3] *Quinquennial Report on Education in Assam*, 1897–1901, para. 46.

cious combination of fortune-telling and pedagogy. In other parts of the same province he is sometimes found practising a dubious kind of medicine. As the supreme representative of enlightenment in the village his services are requisitioned for writing letters, for deciphering knotty legal documents, and for copying deeds.[1] In schools which still maintain their connection with a temple or a mosque, he has his many religious duties to perform. Mr. Adam's description of the subsidiary functions of a *Mulla* teacher still holds good with regard to the class of schools to which it relates. "The *Mullas*, besides teaching a few pupils, the formal reading of a portion of the Koran, perform the marriage ceremony, for which they are paid from one to eight annas according to the means of the party; and also the funeral service with prayers for the dead, continued from one to forty days, for which they get from two annas to one rupee. . . . The *Mullas* also often perform the office of the village butcher, killing animals for food with the usual religious forms, without which their flesh cannot be eaten by Muhammadans; but for this they take no remuneration.[2]

20. Besides these customary offices, Government have frequently found it useful to employ the schoolmaster in village offices of a formal character where his special position in the community is likely to prove advantageous. The arrangement has helped both the schoolmaster and the village community. To the master it has been a means of adding to his rather attenuated emoluments and, at the same time, of reviving his immemorial standing with the community, which the disorganization of the old village life has tended to weaken, while to the villagers his unique qualification for the offices in question has meant a less expensive and more efficient discharge of certain public services in the village. The chief office thus held by

[1] *Eastern Bengal and Assam, Annual Report on Education*, 1905–6, p. 19.
[2] *Report*, p. 105.

the schoolmaster is that of village postmaster, in which, from all accounts, he has proved an almost unquestioned success wherever the experiment has been tried. It will be seen that in remote villages where, amid a dense mass of ignorance, the teacher towers aloft as the recognized symbol of light and leading, the tangled work of deciphering a postal address and of elucidating an occasional notice from the town post office is safest in the hands of this custodian of village enlightenment. The system is found to exist in every province with the possible exception of Assam, and on the whole the verdict of educational officers has been in favour of its continuance. An improvement upon the system has been attempted in Sind, where the schoolmaster, besides holding charge of the post office, is required to give tuition once every week to his pupils in the working of the office.[1] Mr. H. Sharp, C.I.E., the writer of the *Sixth Quinquennial Report on Indian Education* (1907–12), says on the subject: "Throughout a long period of school inspection, the present writer has found but one instance where postal work has seriously interfered with teaching. The case was a peculiar one, where the village, though remote, was a large centre of local trade . . . and the postal work was peculiarly heavy. Elsewhere, he has found that the two duties can be discharged satisfactorily together, and that the school which is also a branch post office is generally among the best conducted."[2] Other public offices sometimes filled by schoolmasters are the management of cattle pounds,[3] and in times of famine the superintendence of relief kitchens started in stricken areas.[4] In the latter case, the additional allowance earned by the schoolmaster enables him to keep the school going during periods of acute agricultural strain.

21. It deserves to be noticed that there are cases

[1] *Annual Report on Education in Bombay*, 1902–3, p. 21. [2] Vol. i, p. 123.

[3] *Central Provinces, Annual Report on Education*, 1905–6, p. 19.

[4] *Ibid.*, 1900–1, p. 19.

where the services of some of the ancient officers of the village community, such as the accountant and the watchman, are still directly utilized in the management of the school—an arrangement which undoubtedly helps to make the school an integral part of the village. The accountant's service consists in either teaching, or helping the schoolmaster to teach, the village revenue system, and familiarizing the children with the village map. In the Punjab a system of travelling *patwaris* (accountants) has been tried for the same purpose, with, so far, rather inadequate success.[1] The services of the village *kotwar* (watchman) are used in the Central Provinces to secure a steady attendance at rural schools, part of his duty being "to aid the master by conducting truants to school."[2]

22. An attempt was made in the Bombay Presidency in 1836 to establish a system of village education which would make the schools an essential part of the village organization on the lines of the ancient communal schools—but the process of decay was found to have proceeded so far that the attempt hardly received any encouragement.[3] An officer of the East India Company, Captain Shortrede, then assistant to the Collector of Poona, obtained permission from Government to start village schools in the Purandhar Taluk. The schools were to be housed in the *dharmsalas* or temples of the village; the master in submitting his reports to the educational officers was required to get them countersigned by the *patel* (village headman) and the *kulkarni* (village accountant); and a further step in the same direction was taken by the effort to employ the old village *joshi* (astrologer) to take the place of schoolmaster. The attempt failed, partly for financial reasons and partly because the village servants, including the *joshi*, were unwilling to

[1] *Annual Report on Education in the Punjab*, 1908–9, p. 41.
[2] *Occasional Reports*, i, Sharp, p. 47.
[3] *Indian Education Commission* (1882–3), *Bombay Report*, p. 10.

face the responsibility. It must be said that Bombay was scarcely a suitable spot for this experiment. The disorganization of the ancient schools was more pronounced in Bombay and Central India than anywhere else. "The reign of terror which Pindari and Maratha hordes created at the beginning of last century had swept away the surviving relics of older civilizations. . . . The hereditary *gurus* or *pundits* had not flourished during the period of anarchy. Some had their throats cut, others had fled to more congenial spheres of action, and many had abandoned their profession in disgust or sighed over empty class-rooms." [1] James Thomason, when he was Lieutenant-Governor of the North-West Provinces, proposed a scheme (1846) for starting a school in every village of a certain size supported by an endowment of revenue-free land. "An endowment in land," he said, "is preferable to a money payment, because it gives greater respectability of station than a pecuniary stipend . . . and because it connects the schoolmaster with the community in a way which renders his services more acceptable to them than if he were the paid servant of the Government." The Court of Directors, however, disapproved of the scheme.[2]

23. A hopeful experiment made by the Indian Government in recent years in the way of reviving the old communal spirit of the village has been the introduction of what are known as village school committees. These committees are started generally in connection with schools under the management of District and Local Boards, who delegate to the committees a larger or smaller share of their powers. The committee stands to the village in the relation of a local educational authority, representative but not elective. The appointment of the members, chosen from among the elders of the village, is made, as a

[1] *Occasional Reports*, i, Sharp, p. 129.

[2] *James Thomason*, Sir W. Muir, T. & T. Clark, 1897, p. 80.

rule, by the Taluka Board of the area in which the village is situated, but their action is subject to the approval of the District Board and of the District Magistrate. As a matter of practice, the appointment is made by the Government educational officers who have charge of the locality, whose recommendations are almost invariably accepted by the Local Boards. The idea of a committee is to re-create a sense of local patriotism in regard to the village school. On the one hand it is to make the school a greater reality in the village by enlisting a kind of proprietary interest on the part of the inhabitants in its working and its fortunes; and on the other hand, it is to be an organ of public opinion which will serve as a check on the schoolmaster whenever he is inclined to shirk his duties or do them perfunctorily. The degree of success attained by these schools varies in the different provinces. There is a widespread tendency among inspecting officers to lament the so far discouraging achievements of the village committee system. It is urged that its influence is distinctly obstructive and that committees are more prone to consider the personal defects of teachers than the interests of the school. The probability is that this lamentation is premature. In one province at any rate, namely, the Central Provinces, it has justified in a large measure the expectations of its founders. And the cause of its success here is a proof that in India local institutions of the kind do not altogether fail where a sufficient degree of genuine responsibility is laid upon them, but that they flag and droop where the forms of local autonomy are emptied of real responsibility and power. The unanimous testimony of imperial and provincial reports attributes the success of village school committees in the Central Provinces to the power given to them to utilize the fee collections of the school. This amount of financial responsibility, apparently small but in a village not to be lightly regarded, has acted as a strong force in stimulating interest in local matters.[1]

24. An interesting picture of a school committee in the Central Provinces is given by Mr. Sharp in his *Occasional Reports*, i (para. 7). "Our visit is expected; and some quarter of a mile from our destination we perceive a little group awaiting our arrival. This is the school committee, composed of the village elders; the *malguzar* or landlord of the village steps forward to greet us and introduce the *panch-log* (committee) one by one. The tall gentleman of somewhat military aspect is the Rajput proprietor of a neighbouring village which, having no school of its own, sends its children here; the stout member, whose ears are encircled by two strings of gold plaques and whose bright yellow cap is set rather rakishly on whitening locks, is the local *bania* or merchant whose duties in connection with the school are to teach the boys the mysteries of cash-book and ledger; he of the black garb and spare features is the village accountant or *patwari*, usually of the *kayasth* or writer caste, who maintains the land records and is expected to make the youthful husbandmen understand how fortunate they are, *sua si bona norint*; the rest are substantial tenants whose hard hands and weather-beaten faces proclaim the rigours of their honourable toil."

25. The rules regarding the functions of a school committee vary in different provinces and sometimes in different districts in the same province. But the duties of a typical committee may be stated as follows: (1) to visit the school collectively as well as individually at fixed periods and record their proceedings in a book, (2) to secure regularity of attendance and enforce discipline, (3) to report irregularities, want of accommodation, etc., to the Local Boards, (4) to grant casual leave to the school-

[1] *Fifth Quinquennial Report on Education in India*, 1902–7, vol. i, p. 106.

master for a limited time, and less usually (5) to construct and repair the school building, and (6) to collect popular subscriptions towards the expenses of the school.

26. Before we leave the subject of school committees, it is necessary to mention another experiment in connection with village schools which has been tried recently in the Central Provinces, which is likely, under sympathetic guidance, to have a perceptible effect in strengthening the civic spirit of villages, namely, the introduction of village libraries and societies. The vast majority of the pupils who pass out of village schools relapse into illiteracy within a few years of leaving school, and any *esprit de corps* or desire for learning which the school may have inspired dies away. The effect of libraries and societies is felt in two ways: (1) they help to sustain the work of the school by providing the pupils with materials for reading after they have left school, and (2) they serve as a central meeting-place for the more educated of the villagers and keep alive their interest in the common well-being of the village. The experiment was first made in 1906 by the Deputy-Commissioner of Balaghat, and the Report of 1910 speaks of the existence of libraries in four other districts. The great difficulty in their way is the dearth of suitable vernacular literature—and until that question has been satisfactorily met, the progress of the experiment is bound to be very slow.

27. In respect of village education, Burma stands on a different footing from the other provinces of India. The bulk of the schools are under the management of Buddhist monasteries, which impart religious instruction on strictly orthodox lines. There are also schools under the management of Government and of private lay managers, but their share in rural education is insignificant compared with the monastic schools (*pongyi-kyaung*). The total number of these schools

was estimated in 1912 at 2,352, with an attendance of 73,123, which is considerably more than half the aggregate attendance in primary schools. "In almost every village of any importance there is a monastery, and in the majority of these monasteries the little boys of the neighbourhood learn their letters."[1]

28. The monastic schools may be distinguished into two classes, according as they are registered or unregistered.[2] Schools which have accepted registration are expected to conform to the regulations of the Education Department regarding the subjects they teach in return for a Government grant, but in practice they do not travel beyond the three R's, the monks even in registered schools having shown little relaxation of their aversion to the teaching of science. In the registered schools the monks still follow their ancient routine of instruction, consisting of reading, writing, and repetition of the sacred writings by rote. In these schools no fees are charged, but pupils make presents in kind to the monks. No monk is permitted to accept remuneration in money; and of presents in kind, his choice is strictly limited by the rules of *Vinaya* (discipline) to four forms of assistance—food, medicine, shelter, and a robe. It is not to be supposed that every monastery is a school or that every monk is a teacher. There are monasteries where meditation, mendicancy, and the repetition of the scriptures finish the round of the daily routine and teaching is entirely neglected. But on the whole it may be said that there are enough monastic schools "to meet the needs of the total number of male pupils of school-going age not already attending public institutions."[3] On the possibilities of monasteries as educational institutions, the following words from the *Burma Education Report of* 1912–13 may be quoted: "The reputation of a monastery which gives a good education extends far

[1] *Quinquennial Report on Education in Burma*, 1907–12; Government Resolution.
[2] *Ibid.*, 1902–7, paras. 10–15.
[3] *Ibid.*, 1907–12, p. 28.

beyond the village fence and attracts boys from distant villages. Parents have confidence in the influence of the monastery, and if they had also an assurance of its ability and willingness to give a sound elementary education such as would help the boy to make his way in the world, the *kyaung* would become a quickening power such as it has never been before. The nation has in its monasteries the ideal combination of a secular education in a religious atmosphere, and it would be a thousand pities if it should fail because of the apathy of the monks themselves."[1]

[1] Para. 5.

CHAPTER III

POOR RELIEF

1. It has been said that "India has a poor law, but it is unwritten."[1] In ordinary times there is no state-organized system of poor relief. A great deal of what in other countries would be considered fit subject for state relief is left either to individual charity or to certain informal organizations. Individual charity has perhaps had more to do with the relief of the poor in ordinary circumstances than any organized agency. Almsgiving has always been regarded as a specially sacred obligation in India, and both religious sanction and long-established tradition have helped to make it one of the supreme duties of the individual citizen. Much of this charity is indiscriminate and consists in giving out doles of grain to needy persons who happen to knock at the doors of the well-to-do. The practice is attended by the dangers associated with a system of undiscerning charity, but it has helped at all times to relieve the state of a very considerable part of the obligation of maintaining the poor.

2. Apart from individual charity, the work of poor relief in an Indian village under normal conditions may be said to be distributed between the family, the caste, and the village community. "It is owing to the profound sense which is felt by all classes of the religious duty of succouring, according to their means, the indigent and helpless who have claims on them as

---

[1] *Report of the Indian Famine Commission*, 1880, App. ii, p. 65.

members of the family, the caste, or the town or village that in ordinary times no state measures of relief are needed."[1] Of these, the family is undoubtedly the most important agency of relief; the rules regarding maintenance of relatives under both the Hindu and the Muhammadan systems of law comprehend a wide circle of persons ranging over various degrees and sorts of relationship. The caste, as the next superior organization to the family, has its own arrangements to help the indigent among its members. The term "caste" in this sense means one of the occupational groups who form the numerous inferior castes. It may be defined in the words of Sir Herbert Risley as "a collection of families or groups of families bearing a common name, which usually denotes or is associated with a specific occupation, claiming common descent from a mythical ancestor human or divine, and professing to follow the same traditional calling."[2] It happens that a group of this kind in a particular village is sometimes only a part of a wider community living in a number of different villages, but in the large majority of cases, the caste consciousness is limited by the bounds of the village and its organizations do not extend beyond the village area. Above the family and the caste is the village community, consisting of all the families and all the groups of families living in the village with organizations affecting the village as a whole. It is not to be supposed that the feeling of community in Indian villages in regard to charitable relief as in regard to other matters has survived in its original strength or that in a considerable part of the country it has survived at all. But in any case it is necessary to notice that there are relics of the old organization to be found here and there which, however rare and enfeebled, are of sufficient importance to claim our attention.

3. The rules regarding the subject of maintenance

[1] *Report of the Indian Famine Commission*, 1880, part i, para. 187.
[2] *Census of India*, 1901, *General Report*, ch. xi, para. 817.

under the Hindu law are intimately associated with the conception of the joint family. "The family would generally be composed of a man, his wife, his unmarried children, his married sons and their wives and children, and in cases where they are not maintained by their husband's family, his widowed daughters."[1] This kind of family might be part of a larger whole, the larger family consisting of "all the descendants in the male line from a common ancestor and their wives, sons and unmarried daughters. Whether the family be of the larger or smaller type, the members would ordinarily live together, being maintained from the common purse, and performing jointly the ceremonies required by their religion."[2] In other words, those who would be entitled to share in the bulk of the family property may claim all their necessary expenses to be paid out of its income. The term "necessary expenses" has been held to include maintenance for the individual member, his wife and his children, and for such persons as he is legally or morally bound to support, and provision for all usual and proper religious observances . . . also provision for the education of his sons and for the marriage expenses of his daughters, or of other female dependents of his family.[3] But the right of maintenance goes farther than this. It extends also to those members of the joint family who, on account of any bodily or mental defect, have been disqualified from inheriting, to illegitimate sons, persons taken in adoption but deprived of their rights by the subsequent birth of a legitimate son, concubines or female slaves . . . widows of the members of the family, and the parents, including the stepmother and mother-in-law.[4] This duty of a householder to maintain the dependent members of his family has always been recognized as a paramount

[1] *Hindu Family Law*, E. J. Trevelyan, 1908, ch. vi, p. 224.
[2] *Ibid.* [3] *Ibid.*, ch. vi, p. 242.
[4] *The Hindu Law*, A. C. Mitra, 1895, p. 186.

obligation, even religious sacrifices being supposed to lose their effect "if thereby a man deprives himself of the means of maintaining his dependents."[1] The injunction in the Code of Manu, from which the whole law of maintenance is derived, is uncompromising in its demand. "The mother and father in their old age, a virtuous wife and an infant son must be maintained, *even though by doing a hundred times that which ought not to be done.*"

4. Under the Muhammadan law, the duty of maintenance, though extensive enough, is less imperative and more restricted than under the Hindu law. Children have of course a right of maintenance against parents, which in the case of a boy continues until he is able to earn his livelihood, or if he is disabled so long as his disability lasts, and in the case of a girl until she is married. As regards other relations, those who are entitled to maintenance must fall within the prohibited degrees of relationship under the law of marriage. The rule with regard to prohibited degrees is as follows: By reason of consanguinity a man cannot marry any female ascendant or descendant of his or the daughter of any ascendant how high soever, or of any descendant how low soever, or the daughter of his brother or sister or the daughter of a brother's or sister's daughter and so on.[2] The duty of an individual to support poor relations, unless they happen to be parents or grandparents, is limited by two conditions, first that he is in easy circumstances himself, second that the relative concerned is helpless by reason of infancy or infirmity or is an unmarried or widowed female.[3] The claim to maintenance is enforced in the order of proximity of the relationship.

[1] *Commentaries on the Hindu Law*, J. W. Bhattacharya, part viii, ch. i, p. 396 (1893).

[2] *Muhammadan Jurisprudence*, Abdur Rahim, ch. viii, 1907 (Tagore Law Lectures).

[3] *Ibid.*

5. The customary form in which a *caste* relieves its poor is by feeding them at the expense of the Caste Fund. This fund is made up almost invariably of fines imposed upon members who infringe the rules of the caste relating to social intercourse, religious duties, etc. The adjudication of social and religious questions among the members of a caste is in the hands of a *panchayat*, which is either a committee of the caste for judicial purposes or is the caste itself assembled to consider disputes among its members. In either case the award of a *panchayat*, at any rate among the inferior castes, has all the sanction of a judicial award, and the fines are as a rule regularly collected. A defaulter is liable to excommunication, which, on account of the social and religious disabilities connected with it, is looked upon as a dreadful form of penalty. In some castes we find, besides fines, certain special imposts levied to augment the caste fund. An interesting case of such special contribution is found among the barber caste (*Ambattans*) of the Madras Presidency, who levy a communal tax of 2½ annas on each family and a contribution of rice on every occasion of a marriage in the caste.[1] In Western India it is sometimes found that a caste raises its fund by taxing articles of trade, sales and mortgages of houses, and marriage booths.[2]

6. The duty of administering charity among the members of a caste is discharged either by the headman assisted by the leading castemen, or through the agency of the temple or mosque with which the caste is connected. Indeed it often happens that a definite portion of the fines collected by a caste and intended by it for charitable purposes is directly handed over to the priest to be used by him in benevolent works. The proportion of the fine which goes to the temple or mosque differs in different castes. Among the

[1] *Castes and Tribes of Southern India*, E. Thurston, vol. i, p. 36.
[2] *Census of India*, 1911, vol. xvi, part i, p. 254.

Paraiyan caste in Madras, the proportion is fixed at a fifth.[1] A general arrangement which obtains among various castes in Bellary (Madras Presidency) is to divide the fine into three parts—one for the priest, one for the members of the *panchayat*, and the third for the *Sirkar* (State).[2] Where the caste itself undertakes to feed the poor, it is usually carried out by the institution of feeding-houses where travellers and others in need are fed free of charge.

7. It is impossible from the materials which we possess to gather a full or connected account of the arrangements by which a village as such maintained its poor in the flourishing days of the village community. We know from evidences which have survived that two institutions which have had the responsibility of looking after the poor of a village, that is, of feeding them with more or less regularity though with no attempt to discriminate between the deserving and undeserving, have been the village temple and the village almshouse, wherever the latter existed as a separate institution. It was the custom under the Hindu governments to provide for the support of these institutions by granting them the revenue on specific portions of land and sometimes by the grant of land itself.[3] These grants were called in some parts *inams* or rewards. In some cases they were supplemented out of benevolences or contributions levied to meet the general expenses of the village (*grāma kharch*)[4] among which the maintenance of the temple and the almshouse was recognized as of supreme importance.[5] In Western and Central India during the period of Maratha rule, the maintenance of the village temple, with its annual and occasional charities, was recognized as *Salabad*, that is, among the permanent expenses of the village and met

[1] *Castes and Tribes of Southern India*, E. Thurston, vol. vi, p. 90.
[2] *Madras District Gazetteer*, Bellary, vol. i, p. 66.
[3] *Land Systems of British India*, Baden-Powell, vol. iii, p. 78.
[4] *Grāma*=village, *kharch*=expense.
[5] *Fifth Report of the Select Committee on East India Affairs*, 1812, p. 129.

by permanent assessments on land. Other village expenses were contingent or *Sadir warid* and met by extra assessments.[1] As a rule, the right of free feeding was restricted to pilgrims and holy men, but it seems probable that this category covered a much wider class than the strict meaning of the words would suggest.[2]

8. Besides these regular institutions of charity, it was not uncommon for beggars to be assigned a definite portion of the harvest from the threshing-floor in the traditional manner of village payments for communal purposes. Relics of this practice are still to be found—for example, in the Hoshiarpur district in the Punjab.[3] That a somewhat analogous custom prevailed also in South India is evidenced by an entry in the *Private Diary of Anandaranga Pillay*.[4] The French Governor ordered certain paddy merchants to bring their supplies of grain to the town and store them up in the market. The merchants protested that before doing so it was necessary, according to custom, to set apart a fourth of the grain for mendicants. "It was a long-standing custom to devote (a fourth) to charity, and if beggars were actually present they were given something by way of alms. The Governor thereupon directed that in future the paddy merchants should not be compelled to part with any portion of their grain, either for mendicants or for charitable purposes, it being entirely left to them to contribute anything that they might think fit.

9. Among the surviving relics of the old communal fund which was raised by a village to meet its general

[1] *Report on the Territories Conquered from the Paishwa*, Elphinstone, p. 26.

[2] The following occurs in the Mysore Revenue Regulations of the time of Tippu Sultan. "The ryots of villages are accustomed to expend their money upon travellers and in celebrating festivals; they are now forbidden to spend their money upon travellers; and it is ordered that when ryots are desirous of expending money in this way, they shall only be allowed to expend one *pagoda* out of one hundred in every village; there is no occasion for them to spend more" (art. 43. Translated by B. Crisp, Calcutta, 1792).

[3] *Punjab District Gazetteers*, Hoshiarpur, p. 174.

[4] Vol. ii, p. 5.

expenses, including the feeding of its poor, perhaps the most important is what is known as *Malba*, still found in certain districts in the Punjab and the United Provinces. In former times the main sources from which this fund was collected were the following: (1) receipts from sale of produce of the common land and rents paid for cultivation of it; (2) a cess levied on the houses of the artisans and sometimes of the shop-keepers at the rate generally of one rupee per annum on each shop or house; (3) a portion of the receipts made by the village weighman.[1] It was an impost which was liable to great abuse on account of the opportunities for extortion which it offered to the representatives of the Central Government who came round collecting the revenue. In his report of the first revenue settlement of the Jullundur district in the Punjab, Sir Richard Temple, speaking of *Malba*, said: "Besides these (i.e. various Government cesses) there were the necessary subscriptions for village expenditure or the illegal gratuities paid to the servants of the Government. All extra imposts were gathered together under the dreaded name of *Malba*. I have heard of the *Malba* in a village equalling the revenue. . . . Grass, wood, timber, fruit, garden produce were all seized upon; to say nothing of the imposts which fell upon the agriculturists in common with the residents of the village. The site of the village could not be removed, no house could be built, no well erected, no plot enclosed, without the payment of a fee."[2]

10. At present the *Malba*, in the form in which it is commonly found, is a cash contribution collected by the village headman from the revenue payers of the village with the first instalment at each harvest. It is a contribution over and above the Government revenue

[1] *Punjab District Gazetteers*, Ludhiana, p. 178.

[2] *Report on the Administration of the Punjab*, 1849–50 and 1850–1. Letter from R. Temple, p. 275.

demand to which it bears a fixed maximum proportion.[1] The administration of the fund is generally in the hands of the headman, but sometimes the duty is assigned to the village shopkeeper (*bania*). It is seldom that any accounts are kept or any explanation of the expenditure is given to the villagers, and the administration of the fund is a frequent cause of dissension in the village. In addition to the usual form of cash contribution, the village fund is still supplemented in some places by the three kinds of receipts mentioned in the foregoing paragraph and sometimes also by taxes on brick-kilns and on marriages.[2] One of the main objects of the fund is the feeding of the poor and of pilgrims, but the administration of the headman is sometimes so lax that individual villagers have to complain of being put to the necessity of feeding people at their houses. Among other public expenses for which the fund is employed are the payment of presents to Government servants, of travelling allowance to village officers and of the cost of providing stationery, etc.

11. Corresponding to the *Malba* in South India is the village communal fund known as *Samudayum* still met with in some of the Tamil-speaking districts of the Madras Presidency. Like the *Malba* it is a surviving relic of the old corporate existence of the village community, and the objects to which its proceeds are devoted are in the main similar. The feeding of the poor is one of the principal objects of the fund, other objects being the repair of village tanks, the erection of drinking water-ponds, and the

[1] E.g. in Hoshiarpur the following maximum rates have been introduced by order of the Commissioner :—

Where the assessment of a village does not exceed Rs. 400, 5 per cent.

Assessment exceeding Rs. 400 and not exceeding Rs. 700, a lump sum of Rs. 20.

Exceeding Rs. 700 and not exceeding Rs. 2,000, 3 per cent.

Over Rs. 2,000, 2 per cent.

Punjab District Gazetteers, Hoshiarpur, p. 183.

[2] *Punjab District Gazetteers*, Jullundur, p. 243.

celebration of festivals at the village temple.[1] The chief sources of the fund are the sale proceeds of the fruits of trees on village land held in common, of the fish in the village tanks, and of the thatching grass which grows on the foreshores of tanks, sometimes also taxes imposed by common consent on articles of certain classes bought or sold in the bazaars.[2] The management of the fund is in the hands of the headman assisted by one or two of the principal villagers. The fund, as a rule, is divided into shares held by descendants of the old leading families in the village (*nattamgars*); and while a considerable part goes towards communal purposes, part has to be divided among the shareholders as their share of the proceeds. These shares are bought and sold and mortgaged like any other property.

12. In a *Punjab District Gazetteer* occurs the following description of a flourishing almshouse (*langar*): "There are two or three famous *langars* or almshouses well-known throughout the country. That of Bagrian lies 40 miles south of Ludhiana and is administered by a resident family of Tarkhans (called Bhais) who hold in *jagir*[3] two or three villages in our territory . . . besides owning a large area of land. Numbers of travellers are fed daily from the public kitchen which is open to all comers, and 1,000 *maunds* of grain are distributed to the public annually. The *dera* or building is a very extensive one—the family has always been in the habit of marrying, and the son succeeds as manager. . . . This *langar* is very well managed. It was kept open in the worst years of drought (1862 and 1868) when the smaller institutions throughout the country were closed, and afforded relief to numbers of the poorer classes in the

[1] *Madras District Gazetteers*, South Arcot, pp. 89–90.
[2] *Ibid.*, Madura, pp. 80–1.
[3] Tenure of land with power to collect the State revenue, and carry on the general administration.

famines of 1897–1900 who flocked to it in search of food."[1]

13. The arrangements described so far relate to the maintenance of the poor in times of normal prosperity. When a famine occurs, these arrangements in most cases break down, and it becomes necessary to summon the aid of the State. The immediate cause of an Indian famine is the failure of the periodic monsoons on which the harvest depends, and when in any year the rains fail or are gravely insufficient, large numbers of the population are faced with the almost certain prospect of starvation and death. The first class of people upon whom an impending famine makes itself felt are the agricultural labourers of the village, whose wages, whether in cash or in kind, depend on the actual out-turn of the harvest. The labourer himself affords to remain at his post for some time after the commencement of the famine, but his dependents are almost immediately thrown adrift and gangs of them begin aimlessly to wander out of the village. Simultaneously with the dependents of agricultural labourers, and perhaps before, large numbers of the idle poor who had been subsisting on the various informal charities of the village are also sent adrift. The contraction of individual and social charity and the consequent wandering of large bodies of villagers constitute the first recognized symptom of an approaching famine. There are few things in the history of Indian Administration during the past thirty years in which the growth of scientific knowledge and the power of organization have achieved a more conspicuous success than the prevention and relief of famines. The elaborate scheme of famine relief which now prevails in India has been the product of successive commissions of inquiry, to report on the results of previous famines and to formulate definite suggestions

[1] *Punjab District Gazetteers*, Ludhiana, pp. 90–1.

for prevention and relief. The whole organization is now set forth in the Famine Codes of the different provinces, of which, in a study of village local government, we must necessarily confine ourselves to that part which relates to the administration of relief through the local institutions and officers of a village.

14. Before proceeding to describe this, it may be of interest to indicate, from such facts as we possess, the course of famine administration in India in ancient times. The *Arthaśāstra* contains the following :—

"During famine, the king shall show favour to his people by providing them with seeds and provisions.

"He may *either* do such works as are usually resorted to in calamities ; he may show favour by distributing either his own collection of provisions or the hoarded income of the rich among the people ; *or* seek for help from his friends among kings.

"Or the policy of thinning the rich by exacting excessive revenue (*Karsanam*) or causing them to vomit their accumulated wealth (*Vamanam*) may be resorted to.

"Or the king with his subjects may emigrate to another kingdom with abundant harvest.

"Or he may remove himself with his subjects to seashores or to the banks of rivers or lakes. He may cause his subjects to grow grains, vegetables, roots and fruits, wherever water is available. He may by hunting and fishing on a large scale provide the people with wild beasts, birds, elephants, tigers or fish.[1]

15. A South Indian inscription sets forth the story of a village which suffered from famine :—

In A.D. 1054, the village of Alangudi (in the Tanjore district) appears to have been afflicted with a famine caused probably by failure of rain. The villagers had consequently no funds to purchase paddy for their own consumption or seed grains and other

[1] *Mysore Review*, April 1909.

things necessary for cultivation. Whatever the cause, the famine-stricken inhabitants of Alangudi could expect no help in their distress from the royal treasury. They had to shift for themselves as best they could. Accordingly they applied to the local temple treasury from which they obtained 1,011 *Kalanju* [1] of gold and 464 *palam* [1] of silver, consisting of temple jewels and vessels. In exchange for this, the members of the village assembly alienated 8¾ *Veli* of land in favour of the god. From the produce of this land the interest on the gold and silver received from the temple was to be paid. Though it is only the payment of interest that is thus provided for, it does not appear that the jewels and vessels were ever to be replaced as such or by an equal weight of gold and silver.[2]

16. Coming to modern times, the necessity for employing the ancient village machinery of India in the relief of distress first received authoritative expression in the *Report of the Indian Famine Commission* of 1880. Previous to the appointment of this Commission, the system had been put to a successful trial in the Behar Famine of 1873-4 by Sir George Campbell and Sir Richard Temple, and by them declared essential for an effective relief of all classes of sufferers. In the years before famine relief was recognized as a state duty, such help as had been organized was the result of private subscriptions and consisted in the erection of poor-houses and relief works in large important centres to which the distressed of every village were expected to repair for help. The system proved very inadequate. The strong feeling of local attachment shown by the average villager, combined with his apathy and his fatalistic notions of life and the caste feeling which deters him from promiscuous association with strangers—all these made it enormously difficult to induce any considerable

[1] Weights which are variously estimated.

[2] *Madras Epigraphy*, *Annual Report*, 1899–1900, p. 20.

number of people to leave their villages and proceed to far-away relief-houses. In these circumstances it was felt neccssary that if any effective relief was to be given, it should be given in the villages close to the homes of the people. This, in its turn, raised the question of a proper organization for ascertaining the actual condition and numbers of the distressed in order as much to eliminate undeserving cases as to include and bring within the area of relief every single deserving case. Into this organization were enlisted all the ancient officers of the village as men who, by immemorial association with the village, were expected to possess the best information on all cases of local suffering.

17. On the question of employing the old village agencies, the Famine Commission of 1880 reported as follows: "In most parts of India some village organization exists which offers a ready and natural, though still imperfect, machinery for coping with famine, and it is of special importance that whatever is possible should be done towards improving and strengthening this machinery where it is present, so that it may become more thoroughly efficient for the purposes of village relief. For the future progress of the country, the encouragement of the principle of local self-government by which business of all kinds should be left more and more to local direction, is of much moment, and nowhere more so than in dealing with local distress; and however great be the difficulties in the way of its early practical realization, it will be well never to lose the opportunity of taking any step that may lead towards it."[1] Sir Richard Temple, who had perhaps more experience of famine administration than any officer before or since his time, in giving evidence before the Commission, mentioned as one of the essential precautions against famine mortality "the enlisting into relief service of all the ancient village

[1] *Report of the Indian Famine Commission*, 1880, part i, para. 142.

institutions of the country." Of village officers, he said: "They are hereditary officers accustomed for generations to perform duties cognate more or less to those of famine relief. They have necessarily a complete knowledge of every family in the village. In most cases they have no motive to do otherwise than right, though like many others they will shirk extreme exertion in critical times unless they are closely supervised. But wherever they have behaved badly as a body, the fault must be either with the collector or his subordinates." [1]

18. Famine relief in a village is given either gratuitously, that is, by free distribution of grain or cooked food, or cash to destitute persons unable to work, or in the shape of wages in return for work done upon village relief works. The agencies of village local government through whom these forms of relief are administered are (1), a committee or *panchayat* specially constituted for the purpose in every village of suitable size, consisting of representative leading men, landowners and cultivators, and (2), the three principal village officers—the headman, the accountant, and the watchman. To these may be added the village grain-dealer or *bania*, who, though he does not hold a formal place on the village staff, is yet a person of great importance in famine times. The work of these village agencies is very closely supervised by a Government officer set in charge of a circle of villages, whose duty is to travel round each village as frequently as possible to stimulate, instruct, check, and personally assist in local activities, and generally to form a channel of communication between the village and the collector and his subordinates. Whenever the provincial Government declares the existence of famine conditions, it is the duty of the collector to set this village machinery in motion by appointing circle officers and village

[1] *Report of the Indian Famine Commission*, 1880, App. ii, p. 51.

committees and by instructing the village officers in their new duties.

19. A great part of the relief in which village institutions are utilized is the gratuitous relief of the infirm and the disabled. The necessity for a thorough local knowledge for the prevention of abuses is of course obvious in the case of any free system of relief, and the policy of Government has been to depend on the knowledge of village officers in regard to each individual case rather than on any general self-acting test.[1] The following are the classes of persons who are eligible for gratuitous village relief, provided they have no relatives able, and by the custom of the country bound, to support them: (*a*) idiots and lunatics, (*b*) cripples, (*c*) blind persons, (*d*) all persons who from age or physical infirmity are incapable of earning their living, (*e*) all persons whose attendance on the sick or on infant children in their own homes is absolutely necessary, (*f*) women of respectable birth who are debarred by national custom from appearing in public, and are unable to provide themselves with sufficient food, (*g*) men of respectable birth who are unable to earn a livelihood and are in danger of starvation.[2] A list of such persons is prepared in each village by the headman or the accountant, assisted by the village committee, and this list is carefully scrutinized by the circle officer during his frequent inspections of the village by local verification and by personal examination of the village officers and the village committee. The relief is given either in cash allowances or in cooked or uncooked rations, more commonly the former. When cash allowances are given, a permanent advance is made to the headman or other village authority sufficient ordinarily for a

[1] Compare the Elberfeld system of Poor Relief.

[2] *United Provinces Famine Code*, para. 137 (1912). Similar provisions exist in other provinces, except Burma, where the absence of the *Zanana* and the caste system renders the last two clauses unnecessary.

month's allowance, which he recoups by bills submitted to the nearest Government treasury. The distributing agency is, at the discretion of the collector, the headman or other officer, the village committee or some individual landowner specially selected.

20. When relief is given in the shape of cooked food, a village kitchen is opened for the purpose with a superintendent in charge. Originally the idea was to restrict cooked food to children and infirm dependents,[1] but it has been found advantageous to extend it to others as well, at least in the later stages of a famine. Its advantage consists in preventing relief being extended stealthily by the recipients to undeserving members of their families, and also in guarding against diseases consequent on ill-cooked food, which sometimes accounts for a considerable share of famine mortality.[2] Those who are thus fed may be employed in light work about the kitchen.[3] When famine is acute or there is a heavy downpour of rain, each village is allowed a kitchen of its own.[4] The system of village kitchens has been found an unsuitable arrangement in Burma, where, on account of the absence of any caste prejudice against inter-eating, cooked food would be very popular and attract immense crowds.[5]

21. When relief takes the form of grain or cooked food, the village moneylender and grain-dealer (*bania* or *mahajan*), as the local purveyor, becomes an important factor. There is no functionary of the Indian village system who has been so persistently attacked as the *bania* or *mahajan*, but in his own way and within limits he has been a potent force in rendering possible the smooth working of the village economy. It is seldom that a cultivator has any accumulated surplus means to carry him from one year to another, and any

[1] *Report of Famine in the Central Provinces*, 1899–1900, vol. i, para. 224.
[2] *Report of Famine in Bombay*, 1899–1902, vol. i, para. 117.
[3] *Bombay Famine Code* (1912), para. 153 (*e*).
[4] *Ibid.*, para. 152, and *Central Provinces Famine Code* (1905), para. 132.
[5] *Report of the Famine Commission*, 1898, para. 164.

capital outlay which he may be called upon to make, such as the repairing of his hut, or the purchasing of a bullock, compels him to secure the assistance of the village moneylender. He is always a willing person, and ready to accommodate, though his terms are not by any means easy. The institution of co-operative credit societies in recent years has tended to displace him from his original position of unquestioned monopoly, but he is still in many villages a man of much influence and importance. Sir J. B. Phear thus described his position in the village economy. "The most usual course of dealing between the parties is this: Such rice grain as is needed by the ryot for sowing or for food, or indeed any other grain, is provided by the *mahajan* on the understanding that it is to be returned together with an addition of 50 per cent. in quantity at the time of harvest, and the money required for purposes immediately connected with the *jote* (or holding of the ryot) is advanced as the occasion occurs, on a like understanding that it is to be repaid at the time of harvest with interest on the loan at the rate of 2 per cent. per mensem for the interval, and that this is to be effected either in the form of an equivalent of rice grain reckoned according to bazaar prices or in cash at the option of the lender. It is not infrequently the case that the *mahajan*, by way of securing the due performance of this arrangement, takes a formal hypothecation of the ryot's future crop and eventually helps himself on the threshing-floor in the open field to the stipulated portion of the produce." [1]

22. In the days before the regular organization of famine relief, as pointed out before, the common method of relieving sufferers was by instituting large relief houses in central places, and the necessary provision of supplies was secured by the establishment of Government granaries. The system was the means of

[1] Paper on *Indian Famines and Village Organization*, East Indian Association, April 11, 1877.

causing great dislocation to private trade, and of throwing out of gear the machinery of village *banias* upon which the economic life of the village in normal times depended. In a strong protest which he wrote to the *Times* in 1873, Sir Bartle Frere, complaining against Government effort to store up grain, said: "An attempt to introduce Government granaries is fatal to the only system of storage which can be really effectual in preserving the surplus of one crop to meet the deficiencies of another—I mean the system of storage by private traders—the much abused Indian *bania*, *mahajan*, or grain-dealer, under whatever name he may be called, is, with all his faults, the only real Pharaoh who in these days can imitate the example of the Egyptian sovereign and his Israelite minister."[1] Under the present organization, the principle is to enlist, wherever possible, the services of the village *bania* for the supply of grain, and where villages are found without a *bania* to group them with other villages which have one. The *Bombay Famine Code*, which deals very fully with this question, has the following provisions: "It shall be the duty of the Relief *Mamlatdar*[2] to fix from time to time the prices to be paid for cleaned grain supplied for the village grain dole . . . and village kitchens. (*a*) The supply of grain shall ordinarily be got in each case from the village *bania* or nearest grain-dealer, if he is willing to supply it at such rates as may be fixed from time to time by the Relief *Mamlatdar*. (*b*) The Relief *Mamlatdar* shall from time to time fix the price of grain for each village in which either a grain-dole is given or a village kitchen is established, and shall take a written agreement from the grain-dealer that he will supply such amount of grain as may be required at the

[1] Quoted in paper on *Famines in India*, by W. Tyler, East India Association, December 18, 1873.

[2] An officer appointed in Bombay to take charge of relief work in a sub-division of a district.

prices fixed by the *Mamlatdar* from time to time, it being part of the agreement (1) that the price fixed by the Relief *Mamlatdar* shall remain in force until altered by him, and (2) that the grain-dealer shall, in the case of a grain-dole, distribute the dole daily, and in the case of a kitchen deliver the amount of grain indented for by the Superintendent daily at the kitchen.[1]

23. While the disabled and the infirm are thus provided for gratuitously in the village itself, the able-bodied are expected ordinarily to find work in the large central relief works. But it has been found necessary also to provide small relief works in the village close to the homes of the people, with the headman or other local authority in charge of them. This class of works has proved specially useful with regard to the small peasant proprietors and tenants, as distinct from the agricultural labourers. The latter are accustomed in search of work to go far out of their villages, but the small landowner or tenant is a person of delicate sensibilities who, when his time comes in the course of a famine to throw up his farm, often risks death rather than face "the odium of enforced companionship with strangers and exposure of their womankind to the familiarities of all kinds of men gathered together at a relief camp."[2] The kind of works included under the term "village works" are the construction and repair of wells, tanks, reservoirs and irrigation channels, the embankment of fields, the removal of noxious weeds from fields, the improvement of village roads and village sites and of the general sanitary condition of the village. The chief advantages of a system of village relief works, as proved by the history of famine administration, may be summarized as follows: (1) It provides employment

[1] *Bombay Famine Code* (1912), para. 155.

[2] *Report of the Famine Commission*, 1898, vol. vii, pp. 43–5. Note on Village Works, by B. K. Bose, C.I.E.

in areas which are situated at a great distance from central relief works. (2) It affords a stop-gap while large works are being organized, and on their dissolution it helps a gradual transition to normal times.[1] (3) It is of "incalculable value" in enlisting the co-operation of village officers and leading men.[2] (4) It is more economical, being managed by local men who have no interest in the work. (5) The retention of people near their homes enables them to take advantage of any temporary means of livelihood that may arise.[3] (6) It helps to carry forward some necessary works of village improvement.

24. Village works fall into two classes, according to the way in which they are managed. Either they are under the control of the collector, a piece of departmental work, or they are under private management, receiving in some cases a grant from the Government. In the latter case, the usual arrangement is for the collector to encourage in advance agreements with influential landowners of the village (who may be the village headmen) with regard to their responsibility for the cost and erection of village works.[4] If the work comes under the class of "aided," an advance loan is made by Government to the landowner on specially favourable terms. The execution of the work is left substantially in his hands subject to the terms of the agreement. The agreement insists upon some such conditions as these—that only the really needy are employed, that rates are paid on a rough piece-work system at rates fixed by the collector, and that periodic returns are submitted as to the numbers employed.[5] Where, on the other hand, the work is under the control of the collector, it is carried out under

[1] *United Provinces Famine Code* (1912), para. 156.

[2] *Report of Famine in the Central Provinces*, 1899–1900, vol. i, para. 82.

[3] *Report of Famine in Bombay*, 1899–1902, vol. i, para. 71.

[4] *United Provinces Famine Code* (1912), para. 25 (*a*). Similar provision in other provinces.

[5] *Report of Famine in the Central Provinces*, 1899–1900, vol. i, para. 164.

the supervision of a minor public works officer of the Government, such as a sub-overseer or a special village works inspector, but even here the immediate agency through whom the work is executed is the village headman or the village relief committee or some individual member of the Committee.[1] Admission to the works is conditional on the production of a permit from the headman or committee of the village.

25. Apart from the specific duties described above, the Famine Codes impose upon village officers duties of a general character. Upon the headman lies the duty of helping in all possible ways the officers of Government in their duties appertaining to famine relief. He is required to keep the *Tahsildar*[2] and the Circle Inspector informed of the general condition of his village, of the state of health, the condition of the cattle, the amount of water-supply, the storage of grain, the number of persons requiring relief, the appearance of starving wanderers, etc.[3] The accountant's duties, which are mostly of a ministerial character, consist in maintaining systematic records of all facts affecting the economic and industrial life of the village. He is, in fact, the headman's clerk, and his work, as the primary collector of statistics in India, is of great importance not merely in the relief of famine but in all questions of general revenue administration. The village watchman is required to patrol the village and the roads leading to it, to inform the people where relief works are carried on or poor-houses established.[4] It is his duty also where a starving wanderer is too weak to walk to assist in carrying him to the place of relief, and in urgent cases he may incur on his own responsibility any expense required.[5] An important problem

[1] *United Provinces Famine Code* (1912), para. 122 (*a*). Similar provision in other provinces.

[2] An officer in charge of a sub-division of a district, exercising both executive and magisterial powers.

[3] *Madras Famine Code* (1905), sec. 3; *Punjab Famine Code* (1905), sec. 90.

[4] *Punjab Famine Code* (1905), sec. 93.

[5] *United Provinces Police Regulations*, ch. 25, sec. 280.

which arises in every village when a famine occurs is how, in face of the general scarcity, to maintain the village servants at their posts and keep them from wandering like the mass of the villagers. Their emoluments, where they are paid by the villagers themselves, as is often the case, are paid in kind, and when there is a general failure of the crops, such payment of course rapidly ceases. It is an interesting fact that in the Central Provinces, where it is the custom to pay the watchman in hides, instead of a drop in wages, the abnormal mortality of cattle helps him to earn a bigger income than ever during the occurrence of a famine.[1] This, however, is exceptional. The general problem is met in every province by placing the village servants concerned (generally the watchman, rarely the accountant) on the village gratuitous relief list and giving them an allowance of grain or cash sufficient to make a subsistence, *less* any emoluments actually received by them by way of ordinary perquisites.[2] Their wives and children, if fit for work, are sent for employment to the village works.[3] In Bombay during the famine of 1905–6, the number of village servants relieved in this manner was in one district (Poona) greater than that of the infirm who received gratuitous relief.[4]

26. The assistance rendered by village officers and village committees in the work of famine relief has been variously estimated. It is obvious, if strict departmental standards are applied, that they have not satisfied a high test of efficiency, or fully justified the responsibilities entrusted to them in the selection of cases of relief and the distribution of relief funds. Their usefulness has mainly consisted in supplying information and in carrying out duties of a mechanical

[1] *Report of Famine in the Central Provinces*, 1899–1900, para. 247.
[2] *Bombay Famine Code* (1912), sec. 158 (*c*).
[3] *Resolution on Famine Administration in the United Provinces*, 1907–8, para. 51.
[4] *Report on Famine in Bombay*, 1905–6, para. 17.

character, in which there has been abundant testimony as to their good work. It must be remembered that, as a class, they have been unaccustomed for centuries to the disciplined and strenuous life of an ordered government; and their employment in the vast machinery of Indian Famine Relief has been a courageous and far-seeing experiment. It is an experiment with a distinct educational value, and it is hardly fair to measure on the strength of a thirty years' record the revision of habits formed during an uninterrupted course of centuries. The results of the system must be judged not so much by what has been left undone as by the little here and there which has been actually done and which holds a fair promise of progress. To those who view the question in this spirit, such a verdict, for instance, as the following report on the important system of village relief works in Hissar in the Punjab, will bring encouragement: "The village headman was the officer in charge with no other establishment than a vernacular clerk of the candidate *patwāri* (village accountant) stamp. . . . The position assigned to the village headman was rarely abused . . . the villagers showing a readiness to co-operate loyally in carrying out the intentions of the Government." [1]

[1] *Report of Famine in Punjab*, 1896–7, para. 58.

CHAPTER IV

SANITATION

1. So far as the idea of public health was present in any form in the village community, it may be said to have been carried out by means, possibly among others, of the physician, the midwife, the scavenger, and the priest and astrologer.

2. Of the physician and midwife our information is meagre. The physician is mentioned in the *Fifth Report* as one of the regular functionaries of a Madras village, but in the recent descriptions of village services, which appear in the *District Gazetteers* of the different provinces, the physician is scarcely ever mentioned, as holding a definite place on the village staff. It is therefore difficult to say what precisely was his standing in the community, whether he was regarded as a casual servant, employed and paid for the occasion, or whether he was remunerated by allotments of grain from the threshing-floor, and looked upon as a public functionary. Some of the early books lay down detailed rules for regulating the practice of medicine and the conduct of physicians, which seem to suggest that the status of the physician was more than merely casual. He was to appear with his medicines whenever there was pestilence abroad, and unskilful handling of cases was to be accounted to him as an offence. The *Arthaśāstra* says: "Physicians undertaking medical treatment without intimating (to the Government) the dangerous nature of the disease shall,

if the patient dies, be punished with the first amercement. If the death of a patient under treatment is due to carelessness in the treatment, the physician shall be punished with the middlemost amercement. Growth of disease due to the negligence or indifference of a physician shall be regarded as assault or violence."[1] In some villages the duties of physician are found combined in the schoolmaster, and more commonly in the barber. It is, perhaps, his association with disease which leads him to be mentioned in the Code of Manu among the persons whose sight is to be avoided at sacred obsequies.[2]

3. Of the village midwife, the information is still more indefinite. There is no reference to her, either in the documents or in the old books under review here, which helps us to fix her place, if she has any, in relation to the village staff. The probability is that her services were hired for the occasion, by anyone who required them, and there was nothing like a formal bond between her and the community. But that she takes even to this day a considerable part in the treatment of maternity cases in India—often to the great detriment of the rising generation—is a fact only too well known to medical practitioners. The superintendent of the Maternity Hospital in Madras,[3] the largest of its kind in India, once speaking of village midwives made this somewhat startling statement: "Midwifery in India is still in an awful condition. It is the common habit and custom in almost all districts to hand over the women in labour to the care of one of the dirtiest, most backward, illiterate, ignorant and superstitious classes, the barber midwife. The result of this custom is that untold misery and unnumbered unnecessary deaths are meted

[1] *Mysore Review*, March 1909.
[2] *Mānava Dharma Sāstra*, ch. iii, sec. 152 (Jones & Haughton).
[3] Lt.-Col. G. G. Giffard, I.M.S. Quoted in *Madras Census Report*, 1911, part i, p. 22.

out to the parturient women of this country, by these untrained and unclean practitioners. I do not exaggerate. Every medical practitioner in this country will substantiate this statement."

4. The actual work of scavenging and of sweeping the lanes and the village site, was entrusted to a menial servant who was retained by the community for the performance of various kinds of general service. This class of village servants have furnished the material in most provinces for the useful body of rural policemen.[1] Their duties are multifarious, of which menial sanitary service forms not the least important part. They sweep the lanes and remove impurities, keep the village meeting-house clean, patrol the village at night, act as messengers to the headmen, serve as referees on matters affecting the village boundaries, guard the crops, assist in agricultural operations, attend on Government officials who visit the village, and carry palanquins and torches at festivals. As a rule they are menials of the lowest caste, and take up their residence on the outskirts of the village.[2]

5. A sanitary requirement for which in many parts of India special provision is made by the village community, is the removal of carcases of dead animals from the village area. In times of famine and pestilence, when cattle mortality occurs in large numbers, the usefulness of the provision is manifest. The duty is left in the hands of the general village servant, but whenever he is in charge of it, he is found generally to be also the bootmaker and leather worker of the village. This combination of functions has its advantage, since for his service in removing dead cattle often the customary mode of payment is the skins of the animals themselves, which serve at the

[1] They are called by different names in different parts of India—*Talayari*, *Toti*, *Vetti* in South India; *Mahar*, *Chamar* in Bombay and Central India; *Musalli*, *Barwala*, *Batwal* in Upper India.

[2] The resemblance of the village watchman to the parish beadle in England will be noticed. See Webb, *The Parish and the County*, pp. 126–7.

same time as raw material for his trade. The service, however, is looked upon as particularly degrading, and often a division has to be effected among village menials, of those who perform the superior duty of looking after the general cleanliness of the village from those who have to remove dead animals.[1] The right to take the skin of the animal has been recently questioned in the Central Provinces, and the civil courts appear to have rejected the claim. In any case the claim is never put forward or enforced where the animal belongs to the village officers or their agnatic relations.[2] A custom has been noticed in the Raipur District of the Central Provinces by which the village servant is offered by the landlord a field free of rent or definite portions of seed grain for removing dead cattle, and in return he is expected to supply shoes free of cost to the landlord and his children twice a year, and give him the neck-ropes and thongs required for his plough-cattle.[3]

6. The number of menials employed in a village varies in different areas, and sometimes in different villages within the same area. The general rule, apparently, is to find more than one. Elphinstone in his Report on the Deccan noticed in each village no fewer than four or five, the number varying according as the original families had branched out.[4] In the Central Provinces the number varies in most villages between two and fifteen, and in the largest villages perhaps still more are found.[5] The remuneration paid to these servants usually takes the form of a fixed proportion of the harvest. It has been calculated in the Central Provinces that the total of the grain contributions in a year, works out in money value

[1] In Madras the *Talayari* is the superior class, and the *Vetti* the inferior. Cf. *Kamdari* and *Bigari Mahars* in the Central Provinces.

[2] *Central Provinces and Berar District Gazetteers*, Akola, pp. 200–2.

[3] *Ibid.*, Raipur, pp. 174–5.

[4] *Report on the Territories Conquered from the Paishwa*, Elphinstone, p. 20.

[5] *Central Provinces and Berar District Gazetteers*, Akola, pp. 200–2.

to an average of Rs. 50 or 60 per man.[1] In Attock in the Punjab the share which goes to the sweeper is about one per cent. of the gross produce. If, in addition to his other duties, he is called in to help in the reaping, his allowance is raised to from five to six per cent. of the total produce.[2] In Nasirabad in Baluchistan the sweeper who, as elsewhere in India, is paid by grain-fees, is estimated to receive in value about Rs. 3 per mensem in addition to his food.[3]

7. That in the villages of ancient Hindu kingdoms the necessity for prescribing certain sanitary rules was realized is evident from scattered references in such books as the *Mahabhārata*, the *Arthas'āstra*, and the Code of Manu. The directions on the subject are of a minute character, and often enter into intimate personal details. The *Mahabharata* prohibits the commission of sanitary malpractices "on a field where crops are grown, or too near an inhabited village, or on a piece of water."[4] The Code of Manu has a similar rule in regard to the King's Highway.[5] Provisions of a like character, made by common arrangement, are sometimes found in villages of the present day. According to an authoritative witness before the Decentralization Commission,[6] some village communities in the Punjab are in the habit of laying down rules as to where the heaps of village manure are to be deposited. So in South India the *Vattimas*, a Brahman caste generally met with in the Tanjore district, are known to display a remarkable corporate unity in the sanitary arranemgents which they make for the village on their own initiative.[7]

8. The *Arthas'āstra* throws some light on the steps

[1] *Central Provinces and Berar District Gazetteers*, Akola, pp. 200–2.
[2] *Punjab District Gazetteers*, Attock, pp. 184–5.
[3] *Baluchistan District Gazetteers*, Sibi, pp. 122–4.
[4] *Anucāsanika Parva*, see civ. (Roy).
[5] Ch. ix. 282. Also ch. iv. 45–54.
[6] M. W. Fenton, I.C.S.
[7] *Madras District Gazeteers*, Tanjore, p. 79.

taken when there was a general outbreak of disease. One of the first things to do was to summon "physicians with their medicines and ascetics and prophets with their auspicious and purificatory ceremonials." Various forms of ceremonial are prescribed such as milking cows on cremation or burial grounds, burning the trunk of a corpse, and spending nights in worship and devotion. When there was sickness among cattle, there were other ceremonies to be performed like "waving lights in cow-sheds" and "the worship of family gods." There must have been great trouble in the kingdom from the presence of rats, as these are specially provided against. The chief measures were to let loose cats and mungoose in order to destroy them, and to spread on the ground grain mixed with the milk of poisonous plants to compass their death. In addition to this, ascetics and prophets were to perform auspicious religious acts, and "on full moon days rats may be worshipped." Similar steps were also taken against locusts, birds, and insects.[1] Among the *Oraons*, an aboriginal caste in Chota Nagpur with a vigorous system of village communities, one of the first duties of the *panchayat*, when sickness appears in the village, is to discover the wizard or witch who has caused the disease and make due arrangements for its pacification.[2]

9. The history of modern sanitation in India begins with the appointment by the British Parliament in 1859 of a Royal Commission to inquire into the health of the Indian Army.[3] The Commission presented its Report in 1863, and among its proposals was the appointment for each Presidency of a Com-

[1] *Mysore Review*, April 1909.

[2] *Census of India*, 1911, vol. 5, part i, p. 47.

[3] The general sanitary condition of Indian villages is thus described in the *Imperial Gazetteer of India* (vol. iv, p. 468)—"The village house is still often ill-ventilated and over-populated; the village site dirty, crowded with cattle, choked with rank vegetation, and poisoned by stagnant pools; and the village tanks polluted, and used indiscriminately for bathing, cooking, and drinking."

mission of Public Health, which subsequently was superseded by a single Sanitary Commissioner with a staff of assistants. The reports issued from time to time by these officers and the reviews passed on them by the Army Sanitary Commission in England, resulted in considerably increased attention being devoted to the sanitary condition of rural as well as urban areas. The earliest efforts of Government in village sanitation consisted in the promulgation of rules for enforcing certain elementary sanitary precautions. But these rules did not achieve any substantial progress, partly because there was no proper executive agency to carry them into effect, and partly for lack of funds. The idea of utilizing the ancient village machinery for carrying out the new sanitary programme was first drawn attention to prominently by the Army Sanitary Commission in England in their Review of 1879. The Commission suggested four possible agencies for the sanitary improvement of villages—(1) the inhabitants, (2) the village officers, (3) the village proprietor, and (4) the Government. "The village officer," they said, "where he exists, may help to remove the most important domestic causes of ill-health which afflict the great mass of the people in India. He might take the following steps, and in some way authority might be given him for this purpose. He should see that all the village streets and lanes are kept clean and free of nuisance, that no filth or foul matter is thrown on the surface, and that no one is permitted to perform the offices of nature in any village, street, lane or open space." [1]

10. The first attempt to fix this responsibility upon the village officer by legislation was made in the Central Provinces Land Revenue Act [2] which declared it the duty of the village headman to "keep his

[1] App. II. to Resolution of Government of India, Home Department, 3/212–225, July 27, 1888.

[2] Act xviii. of 1881, sec. 141 (*e*).

village in good sanitary condition, subject to any rules issued by the Chief Commissioner." Rules have now been framed in every province laying certain simple sanitary duties on the village headman, assisted by the other village officers. He is to watch the sources of water supply, the general cleanliness of the village surface, the condition of burial and cremation grounds, the provision of open ground for conservancy purposes, etc. In cases where he is unable, without assistance, to carry out any necessary measure, he is to report to the Revenue Officer of the sub-division in which his village lies.

11. Along with the promulgation of rules, a systematic effort was made in some provinces to educate the headmen and the inhabitants to a sense of the importance of scientific sanitation—without which the rules obviously had little chance of being put to effective operation. The extension of village schools helped in the process, but experiments were also made of a more direct kind. One of the earliest was attempted in 1879 in Banda in the North-West Provinces by a capable District Officer, Mr. McConaghey. His plan apparently was to interest first the village physician by persuasion and coaxing, and through him to work to remove the prejudices of the villagers. He relied also on constant personal interviews with village headmen. "I have always found," he said, "that a great deal can be done by talking to the headmen in their villages and explaining to them why such trouble is taken."[1] The Sanitary Commissioner of the Punjab described his plan thus: "On arrival at a village I send the *Chuprāssie* (or messenger in attendance on me from the Collectorate) to summon the *lambardars*, or headmen, and briefly stating the objects of my visit, inform them that I shall be glad to meet all the principal residents and householders

[1] *Annual Report of the Sanitary Commissioner with the Government of India*, 1879, para. 138.

to explain to them the results of my inspection. At the same time I give directions for the *Chaukidars*, or watchmen, to be summoned and to bring their memorandum books of births and deaths with them, and also to collect the children who have been vaccinated, for my inspection. In a few minutes I have most of the headmen and householders assembled about me, and with them proceed on a tour of the village lanes and courts and the ground about the outskirts, stopping now and then to point out defects and their remedies. I then assemble all at the school or under the tree, and hold a conversation on sanitary matters."[1]

12. A less satisfactory method of enlisting the interest of village officers and the village community—namely, by the grant of rewards—has been tried in a few provinces, particularly in the Punjab. The grants are made by the District Boards, and rules have been framed specifying the points on which stress is to be laid. Water supply, surface cleanliness, and the absence of insanitary hollows are the main things to be considered in the grant of awards.[2] The original intention of Government was to reward village communities as a whole by offering to pay a portion of the revenue demand of the one village in each sub-division of a district which showed the best sanitary results during the year.[3] But the practice has also grown up—partly, no doubt, on the analogy of rewarding individuals who have carried out works of public utility—of spending part of the funds in awarding money grants, badges, and titles to the headmen of village communities. In one of the new Irrigation Settlements in the Punjab, the Chenab Canal Colony, the grants to village communities took the shape of assistance in the construction of mosques, *dharmsalas* and guest-houses, should the villagers with the consent of the Deputy Commissioner desire to expend the rewards

[1] *Sanitary Report, Punjab*, 1880, para. 106.
[2] *Ibid.*, 1900, para. 34.
[3] *Ibid.*, 1898, Orders of Government, para. 16.

on such subjects; and in the year 1908 alone a sum of Rs. 25,740 was utilized in the Colony in grants to village communities and headmen.[1] In either case, whether of awards to communities or to individuals, the system has not made for progress. The official reports speak mainly of the inadequacy of the rewards and the consequent apathy of villagers as the cause of failure, but it is hardly to be expected that an artificial interest in sanitation stimulated by rewards, however tempting, would either be sustained or lead to an appreciation of the importance of sanitation for its own sake.

13. While rules were introduced into villages and efforts made to evoke their interest, a more practical step was taken in many provinces by the appointment on a definite basis of the old hereditary servants who did menial work in the village. The earlier reports of Sanitary Commissioners constantly refer to the need of reviving the customary sanitary service of the village community. The Sanitary Commissioner for Madras in his Report of 1878 said: "Every village has, in theory, one or more sweepers whose public duties ought to be those of scavenger for the whole community, but who do not perform their assigned duties; and it seems only right that some inquiry should be made in regard to the emoluments and position of such servants, and why the original uses of such servants in village life should have been lost sight of."[2] The Bombay Commissioner reported in 1887: "Under the old organization they received from each house-owner for scavenging the village so many handfuls of grain at the time of each crop. This practice . . . has been permitted gradually to fall into disuse, and the consequence is that the village surface no longer receives the partial cleansing it used to do under native rule."[3] And in the Punjab Report of 1895 occurred the

[1] *Sanitary Report, Punjab*, 1908, para. 48. The grants in the Canal Colony have now been withdrawn.

[2] *Sanitary Report, Madras*, 1878, para. 600.

[3] *Sanitary Report, Bombay*, 1887, para. 213.

following reference: "There are usually several people of the sweeper class in the village, and these are more or less the general servants of the villagers and more particularly of the *lambardar*. We have, therefore, ready to hand the agents of good sanitation. It only remains to show the people what is required." [1] A perceptible improvement took place, in consequence, in the position of this class of servants. They were more widely employed—and their remuneration was rendered less precarious by the gradual substitution of money salaries for grain fees. But except in the event of their appointment by the new village organizations, they have lost their sense of responsibility to the village community. Their responsibility has been transferred to the revenue officers of Government or to officers of District and Local Boards.

14. The utilization of the village physician in the new medical and sanitary scheme was the subject of an interesting proposal in the Punjab in 1865–6. It was first introduced in the Sialkot District by the then Deputy Commissioner, and was since extended into other districts.[2] The essence of the scheme was to raise a voluntary tax from the people and spend it on (1) The supply of medicine *gratis*, (2) the pay of village *Hakims*,[3] (3) Scholarships given to deserving young men to enable them to go through some recognized medical school under English training. The rate of assessment was fixed with the consent of the people at an anna and a half per annum per house. The scheme was worked by a non-official committee, either a District or a Local Committee appointed by the District Officer. They chose the *Hakims* by examination, with a due regard to the wishes of the people among whom they are to work. Each *Hakim* had an apprentice attached to him who

[1] *Sanitary Report, Punjab*, 1895, para. 78.
[2] *Administration Report, Punjab*, 1865–6, para. 369.
[3] Indian physicians practising the Muhammadan system of medicine.

might eventually succeed him or take a scholarship.[1] It is not known what the subsequent fate of the experiment has been. The position of village midwives has been also under consideration. In a recent Resolution by the Government of India, the following statement was made on the subject: "Village midwives are, in some districts, encouraged by small grants of money and rewards to attend at the headquarters hospital for a short and simple course of training. These measures open up possibilities with reference to a reduction in infantile mortality and children's diseases generally."[2]

15. The absence of a properly equipped executive agency for rural sanitation was to some extent remedied by the creation of District and Local Boards and Village Unions under the Local Self-Government Acts of 1883–5, and subsequently by the constitution of Village Sanitary Committees in certain provinces under special legislative enactments. One of the primary duties of District and Local Boards was declared to be the sanitary administration of rural areas, and there has undoubtedly been a great advance in sanitary progress since their creation. The progress which has been achieved in recent years by the institution of hospitals and dispensaries and the organization of staffs for vaccination and inoculation, and of sanitary engineers and inspectors is to be traced to the joint labours of Government officers and Local Boards. But these do not fall within the scope of a study of village local government, the areas they administer being great groups of villages between which there is often no stronger bond than the fact that they are included in a common administrative area. Of Village Unions and Village Sanitary Committees we must speak more fully,

[1] For a somewhat analogous scheme in Egypt, see *Report on Finance, Administration, etc., of Egypt*, 1908, p. 370 (Parl. Paper, Cv.).

[2] *Resolution of Government of India*, Nos. 888–908, May 23, 1914, para. 46. For a scheme for utilizing village midwives in Egypt, see *Report on Egypt*, 1913, pp. 10–11 (Parl. Paper, Cd. 7358).

because they form a most interesting experiment by the Legislature for the purpose of utilizing the old communal life of villages in an important object of local government. They are, both of them, "artificial organizations," for which the old village *panchayat* has to a certain extent supplied the model. But while a Sanitary Committee is, as a rule, restricted to the administration of a single village, a Union is a small group of villages situated in closely adjacent areas with sufficient means of easy communication with one another. It would be a useful inquiry whether the corporate feeling of the single village community is sustained when a number of different villages, however closely situated, are linked together, or whether in the process of extension it tends to become too thin and diffuse.

16. Village Unions are found in Madras and Bengal, but in the latter province they have never been an integral part of the system. They are mostly aggregations of villages, not sufficiently large to be constituted into municipalities but important enough to require a local executive agency of their own. Their functions are largely sanitary, but they are also entrusted with the management and lighting of roads and the control of markets and rest-houses.[1] In Madras they work under the immediate direction of the Taluk Board, but in Bengal by an Amending Act in 1908 they have been placed under the direct control of District Boards. The relative progress of the system in Madras and Bengal may be judged from the following statistics in the *Imperial Gazetteer of India*.[2] "In Madras, between 1889–90 and 1902–3, the number of Unions increased from 248 to 379 and their income from 3½ to nearly 7 lakhs of rupees (a lakh = 100,000). . . . In Bengal the Village Union System was introduced experimentally in 1895–6 and the number of Unions

[1] *Administration Report, Madras*, 1911–2, pp. 53–5.

[2] Vol. iv, ch. ix, p. 304.

amounted in 1902–3 to 57. Their average income was only Rs. 493" (or a total of approximately Rs. 23,000). The number of Unions in Madras in 1911–2 was 393,[1] but there has been no progress during the corresponding time in Bengal.[2] It may be pointed out that even the numbers in Madras "do not represent a complete network of petty rural boards, but merely include specially large or important village centres."[3]

17. The administration of a Union is in the hands of a body called by the time-honoured title of *panchayat*, which consists of five or more members (limited in Bengal to nine) who may be either appointed by Government or elected by the taxpayers and inhabitants of the Union.[4] In Madras a scheme for the partial introduction of the elective method of appointment was sanctioned by the Government in 1911–2. The headman of each village included in the Union is an ex-officio member, and the chairman is nominated (in Madras) by the President of the Taluk Board in virtue of powers delegated to him by the Government. The duties of the *panchayat* as laid down in the Madras Act are: (*a*) the lighting of the public roads, (*b*) cleansing of the public roads, drains, tanks, wells, etc., (*c*) with the sanction of the Government, the establishment and maintenance of hospitals, dispensaries, and schools, (*d*) making and repairing the public roads and drains in the Union, (*e*) constructing and repairing such tanks and wells, etc., as will supply the inhabitants of the Union with a sufficient supply of water for domestic use, and (*f*) generally doing such things as may be necessary for the preservation of public health.[5] The Bengal Act provides further for the management of cattle pounds and the control of

[1] *Administration Report, Madras*, 1911–2, p. 146.

[2] The question of reorganizing Village Unions in Bengal was recently the subject of a special inquiry, p. 200, *infra*.

[3] *Report of Royal Commission on Decentralization in India* (1907–9), p. 238.

[4] Madras Local Boards Act v. of 1884, sec. 121. Bengal Local Self-Government Act iii. of 1885, sec. 39 and 41.

[5] Sec. 141.

the registration of vital statistics. The income of Union *Panchayats* in Madras is derived chiefly from a tax on houses. Other sources of income include tolls, fees for the use of markets, cart stands, and slaughter houses, and other miscellaneous fees.[1] In Bengal, under the Act of 1885, the Union Fund was to consist of money accruing under the Cattle Trespass Act and sums assigned as contributions by the Local Government and the District Board. But by the Amending Act of 1908 Union Committees have been empowered to impose a tax to meet the cost of improvements effected by them, if such cost cannot be met from their ordinary income.[2]

18. Since the passing of the Local Self-Government Acts, the Government of India under Lord Dufferin issued in 1888 an important statement of sanitary policy, in which they charged Provincial Governments, where the existing law made no provision or insufficient provision for the enforcement of necessary sanitary measures in rural areas, that "there should be no hesitation in taking the necessary power by legislation."[3] In three provinces where Village Unions had not been formed—Bombay, the Central Provinces, and the United Provinces—the opportunity was taken to pass special Village Sanitation Acts. The result of these Acts in Bombay and the Central Provinces (1889) was to create the system of Village Sanitary Committees. Unlike the Village Unions, their purpose was exclusively sanitary, and was defined in the Statement of Objects and Reasons of the Bombay Act as follows[4]: "The intention is to constitute, wherever necessary, small local authorities who, with the co-operation of the magistracy, will be entrusted with the important duty of attending to village sanita-

---

1 *Administration Report, Madras,* 1911–2, p. 46.
2 Bengal Act v. of 1908, sec. 118 B.
3 *Resolution of Government of India,* July 27, 1888, para. 16.
4 *Bombay Gazette,* 1889, part v, p. 9.

tion. It is thought that without the aid of such local bodies, *operating each within the sphere in which by its constitution it is most likely to possess influence*, to attempt to introduce the minor measures of sanitary improvement, which everywhere beyond the limits of muncipal districts are so urgently needed, will not be successful." The total number of villages in Bombay in which Sanitary Committees had been formed was 286 in 1911–2 and in the Central Provinces 56.[1] The Village Sanitation Act of the United Provinces (1892) was concerned only with the subject of water supply, and it merely empowered the collector to order wells to be cleaned and protected and new wells constructed, the cost being recovered from persons using the well or from the landlord. The question of Village Sanitary Committees was not taken up till 1912, when on the recommendation of the Decentralization Commission the Government decided to make a few experiments.

19. In Bombay, villages were divided into three classes for the purposes of the Act—(1) those in which the inhabitants had taken measures independently for sanitation, (2) small villages in which the needs were few and a simple type of local machinery was sufficient, (3) large villages in which a fairly elaborate system of sanitation was necessary. The first class of villages were left out of the operation of the Act. In villages of the second class, it was open to the collector of the District, at his discretion, to appoint a Sanitary Committee consisting of three or more adult resident householders nominated by him ; and every magistrate, having jurisdiction in the village, could take part in the Committees' proceedings. The Committee was given power to make rules and punish breaches. It could also authorize expenditure and raise the necessary money by voluntary subscriptions or, if

[1] *Administration Report, Bombay*, 1911–2, p. 204 ; *Administration Report, Central Provinces*, 1911–2, p. 95.

required, by a rate assessed by the collector, in conference with the Committee, on the inhabitants of the village. In the third class were appointed what are called Sanitary Boards, partly residents of the village and partly magistrates having jurisdiction in the area, all nominated by the collector, the total number being prescribed by the Government. In addition to the powers possessed by a Sanitary Committee, a Board has authority, with the approval of the collector, to enter into contracts for the daily surface cleaning of the village and to provide for the construction of essential works and buildings. Besides, in a village administered by a Sanitary Board, the collector may appoint a Sanitary Inspector with necessary subordinates, who will be paid by the Board and whose duty will be to prevent breaches of the Board's rules and to bring offenders before the Board for punishment. The only element of popular election allowed in the Act is the provision that in order to aid him in his choice of members, it is open to the collector to procure the election by the householders of the village of qualified persons, in such mode as he shall deem expedient.[1]

20. On a perusal of the Reports on the working of Village Sanitary Committees in Bombay, it is apparent that the system has not given satisfaction to the officers of the Sanitary Department and that in their judgment the influence of the Committees on sanitary progress has been immaterial. When we try to examine the causes of this failure, the Reports reveal, on analysis, what appears to be a contradiction. The Government of Bombay in their Resolution on the Sanitary Report for 1911, said that the shortcomings of the Village Sanitary Committees were "principally attributable to the exiguous nature of their resources. Little in the way of sanitary improvement can be expected from bodies whose average annual expenditure barely

[1] Bombay Act i. of 1889, sec. 8 (1) and sec. 19 (1).

exceeds Rs. 400."[1] Alongside of this statement must be set the financial statistics of the Committees as given in the Report of 1912. The aggregate income of all the Committees in the Province during the year was about Rs. 250,000, out of which there was left a total balance of over Rs. 110,000. When we analyse them by districts, we find of the twenty-six districts at least ten had a balance of over half the gross income and a considerable number over a third.[2] The fact of the matter seems to be that there are two distinct types of villages—one which finds it impossible on a voluntary system of assessment to raise the necessary money, and another which, having raised the money, has not been sufficiently enlightened about the right objects of expenditure. A considerable part of the annual outlay goes to the lighting of the village streets which, in the eyes of many Committees, is of much greater consequence than drainage and water-supply. As a rule, the only form of real sanitary expenditure undertaken by the Committees is the maintenance of a few sweepers in each village. Sir Frederick Lely, who was for several years in the Bombay Civil Service, made the following criticism on the principle of the Act. "I cannot but think a legislature in touch with the people would have included in the Village Act optional provisions enabling the *Panch* (Committee), in lieu of contribution and establishments, to compel each and every householder to keep his house clean, both front and back, by private arrangement with one of the village sweepers, and also to give his quota in labour, if he chose, when any public work had to be done. . . . This would have been working up from ancient village custom instead of down from a foreign and not yet assimilated institution."[3]

---

1 Para. 8.

2 *Sanitary Report, Bombay*, 1912, para. 71.

3 *Suggestions for the Better Governing of India*, Sir F. S. Lely, London, 1906, pp. 84–9.

21. The system of Village Sanitary Committees in the Central Provinces is, in the main, similar to the Bombay system, but a few of the more important differences may be pointed out. The Central Provinces Act, especially as amended in 1902, applies only to large villages, no village of under five hundred houses being allowed to come under the Act.[1] It was expressly stated by Government that the Act was "wholly unsuited to small agricultural hamlets in which sanitary enthusiasm, if untempered by discretion, may easily harass and even injure the people. It is in the local centres of distribution from which the country folk draw their supplies at a weekly market, and in which the need for conservancy is greater, and local public opinion is stronger, that its provisions will be found most useful."[2] As regards the constitution of the Committee, a larger provision is made in the Central Provinces for the elective element. The Committee consists of the headman (*Mukaddam*) and not less than four representatives of the village community "who shall be chosen by election from among the inhabitants of the local area."[3] The election is held in open assembly by owners of houses and proprietors or tenants of land permanently resident within the local area."[4] Moreover, while the assessment under the Bombay Act is mainly voluntary, the Central Provinces Act provides for the necessary funds by compulsory assessment. The principal taxes levied under the Act are an assessment on houses and lands, license-fees on professional weighmen and measurers, tolls on carts, pack animals, and on porters and on animals sold in the village, rents from dealers temporarily occupying open ground in the local area, and lastly, fees on the voluntary registration of cattle sales effected in the village."[5]

[1] Act xi. of 1902, sec. 2.
[2] Speech by the Hon. D. Ibbetson, Imperial Legislative Council, July 18, 1902.
[3] Act xi. of 1902, sec. 3.
[4] *Local Rules and Orders of the Central Provinces*, 1904, pp. 132–8, Rule 5.
[5] Act xi. of 1902, sec. 5.

22. The Report of the Royal Commission on Decentralization (1907–9) marks another stage in the development of village organizations for sanitation. The Commission recommended an extension of Village Committees in areas where they had not been tried.[1] The United Provinces were among the first to act on the recommendation of the commission, but in framing their proposal they declined to regard the measure as a permanent arrangement but looked upon it merely as an experiment. They also decided to circumscribe the sphere of work assigned to the committees under their scheme. They were to be concerned merely with the utilization of funds allotted to them by the District Board; and they were not to carry out any new schemes, however small, but only to maintain the general cleanliness of the village. The Committees would be chosen or approved by the District Board, but in the expenditure of the funds the Committees were to have unfettered freedom. "Any inspection by an official or by a member of the District Board should be with a view to his forming an opinion as to how the scheme has worked, and should not imply any detailed scrutiny of the work done." There are to be no formal accounts and no records. Local subscriptions to supplement the grants of the District Board were to be encouraged but not to be made a condition of the grant. For the present the maximum grant allotted to a village in a year was to be limited to Rs. 50.[2] The United Provinces Sanitary Report for 1913 recognized the experiment as a success in one district, but regarded it as doubtful in the other districts selected.[3] A similar measure was attempted in Assam in the same year, the selected villages receiving their grants from the respective district officers. The experiment was, however, merged in the larger experi-

[1] *Report*, para. 711.
[2] Resolution of United Provinces Government, March 29, 1912.
[3] *Sanitary Report, United Provinces*, 1913, Orders of Government, para. 12.

ment now (1913) on foot in Assam in the organization of village authorities." [1]

23. A system for maintaining an accurate record of the sanitary needs and condition of villages was introduced by the Government of India in 1895 by the institution of what are called Village Sanitary Note Books. These note books, of which each important village is expected to possess one, are to be a permanent record of the sanitary features of the village. The object of the book is primarily to serve as a source of information to the medical and administrative officers of the district, but it serves incidentally, whereever it is maintained conscientiously, to bring home more definitely to the village authorities themselves the sanitary defects of their village. The book is in a printed form, with a series of set questions on such topics as drainage, water supply, disposition of houses, characteristics of the population, conservancy, vital statistics, meteorological conditions, etc. A blank page is left after each set of questions in which Government officers of a required standing who pass through the village are expected to record their remarks. The book is kept in the village itself, in the hands of an influential literate resident, who may be a village officer, a land-owner, the schoolmaster, or in larger villages a Government servant, such as a hospital assistant or an inferior police officer. Once every quarter the books are sent to the civil surgeon of the district for him to abstract any information which may have a bearing on the sanitary administration of the district. The book proved of special advantage in the United Provinces during the famine of 1902, as the information it contained was of great use in determining the kind of relief works likely to be most useful in the villages.[2] While in some provinces the system

[1] *Sanitary Report, Assam*, 1913, Orders of Chief Commissioner, para. 6. A scheme for the organization of village institutions in Assam has now been completed, p. 200, *infra*.

[2] *Sanitary Report, United Provinces*, 1903, Orders of Government, para. 3.

has, on the whole, been justified by the result, the reports have not been unanimous in its commendation. Government officers have not been regular in asking for, and entering their remarks in, the books, and whatever the causes of this indifference, the technical character of the questions, most of which require expert knowledge, may have partly accounted for it.

24. In that important branch of sanitary administration, the registration of births and deaths, village officers throughout India play a conspicuous part. They form in every province the primary agency for collecting facts and for reporting them to the proper recording office. In Bengal, the United Provinces (except the hill tracts), the Punjab, the North-West Frontier Province, and the Central Provinces, the reporting agent is the village policeman. In all other provinces, except Bombay, he is the village headman. In Bombay the duty is divided between the accountant and the village official called the police *patel*, while in Sind the schoolmaster is sometimes found in charge. The recording office, in most cases, is the nearest police station, but in the United Provinces and Bombay the village officers who report the facts also maintain permanent registers for recording them. In Madras the headmen report to the collector, and in Burma they record entries themselves of which copies are made over to the police patrol for submission to police stations.[1] The accuracy of these statistics is checked by officers of the Revenue, Medical and Police Departments, and above all by Inspectors of Vaccination, who are required to make inquiries regarding vital occurrences when on their rounds to test vaccination operations. Nevertheless, the reporting of statistics is still in an unsatisfactory condition, it having been noticed in Bengal alone that as many as 30 per cent. of the deaths and 52 per cent. of the births have been

[1] *Report of Sanitary Commissioner with the Government of India*, 1905, p. 98 (Tabular Statement).

unrecorded.[1] The illiteracy of the village officers is the principal difficulty. The prejudice of caste, the ill-luck supposed to attend enumeration, the comparative ignoring of female births and deaths as matters of little consequence—these are other hindrances. In regard to death statistics, apart from inaccuracy of numbers, the statement of the causes of deaths is often of little practical value. Most diseases are described as "fevers" or "bowel complaints," the village officer being incapable of any profounder diagnosis.

25. A description of village sanitary institutions in India will not be complete without a reference to the unofficial associations which have been set up here and there in the course of the last thirty years, under the familiar title of *panchayat*, for the promotion of sanitation. They do not owe their initiation to legislative or official action, though in the course of their development they have received active support from Government; nor is it possible to trace any definite connection between them and the old village community. They are generally private enterprises, due to the spread of education and the growth of a new public spirit, but it is conceivable that they have been helped by local traditions of the old corporate unity. So long ago as 1881, it was noted in Bengal that in several populous villages where pleaders and retired servants of Government had settled down, informal *panchayats* had sprung up, which "built culverts, made roads, and drained dirty places, all with funds freely contributed by the villagers."[2] A *panchayat* in a village in the United Provinces was officially reported in 1912, "consisting of two respectable *vakils* (pleaders), and the headman and two *banias*. . . . A sum of about Rs. 150 was raised by subscription, and two sweepers on Rs. 3 each

[1] Paper on "Vital Statistics," by Dr. C. A. Bentley, 3rd All India Sanitary Conference, January 1914.

[2] *Report of Sanitary Commissioner with the Government of India*, 1881, para. 189.

a month were appointed, and a receptacle of iron for carrying dirty water out of the village was purchased. . . . The fourteen wells in the village were cleaned. . . ."[1] The Madras Government, in a recent order surveying the voluntary activities of villages in sanitation, said: "In many districts, a piece of communal land away from the village site is set apart for the storage of manure; in others, areas are set apart for use as latrines to prevent the indiscriminate fouling of the whole surroundings of the village; in some districts, village 'Sanitary Associations' have been in existence, which administer a voluntary cess raised by the people themselves for maintaining scavengers; in others, the villagers have subscribed regularly towards the cost of pumping water from protected wells to raised cisterns."[2] The most interesting instance of independent action in rural sanitation is reported from Bombay, in connection with the Florence Nightingale Fund for the Promotion of Village Sanitation in India. "The Committee adopted an admirable scheme . . . . based on the voluntary services of young men and women devoted to the cause of rural health. It was arranged that these Health Missioners should in each case work with a village Committee consisting of the *patel* (headman), *kulkarni* (accountant), and schoolmaster, and two leading villagers; and that they should study the sanitary needs of the people, giving instruction by personal intercourse and magic-lantern lecture, and gradually gaining the confidence of the women, the children, and the depressed classes."[3] The results of the experiment in the few selected villages have been encouraging.

26. Of a similar character is the work which has been begun by village co-operative credit societies. These societies, during the past ten years, have made a

---

[1] *Resolution of United Provinces Government*, March 29, 1912, Appendix.
[2] *Madras Weekly Mail*, July 2, 1914, p. 20.
[3] *India*, London, July 10, 1914, p. 16. Letter from Sir W. Wedderburn.

remarkable progress in India, and as in most countries where the movement has spread, the economic advantages have been supplemented by the social and moral benefits which have flowed from it. Sanitation is one of the objects which have claimed most attention from the promoters of village co-operative societies. A recent Conference of co-operative societies in a Madras District passed the following Resolution : "It is the opinion of this Conference that Local Boards should make use of the agency of co-operative societies for improving village sanitation and village communication."[1] The Resolution may be taken as sufficiently typical. In many parts of India the co-operative movement has been hailed by responsible administrators as marking the dawn of a new era of village communal life, and it is a great deal to the good that outside their proper economic sphere this new life has been manifested in the hitherto neglected field of sanitation.

[1] *Tanjore District Co-operative Conference*, January 1914.

CHAPTER V

PUBLIC WORKS

1. THE arrangements made by the village community for the erection and maintenance of its public works, such as wells, tanks, channels, roads, and buildings, constitute a notable feature of village local government. The most important of these works, to which the community has always devoted special attention, as is to be expected in a country so predominantly agricultural, is the maintenance of a sufficient water supply for agricultural as well as domestic purposes. In all provinces where the condition of the land has called for irrigation, some kind of a systematic arrangement has been set up by custom, in many cases to be traced to remote times, not merely for making and maintaining tanks and channels, but for distributing the water and settling disputes arising out of it. A usual element in these arrangements is the institution of village communal labour, by which each member of the community is required to contribute his share of the labour or expense required for the upkeep of the works in his village. A long controversy has been carried on, especially in South India, as to how far the custom has survived to our day. The more authoritative opinion in the province has declared for the continuance of the custom, and for its revival in some form. The progress of this controversy has been marked by the production of some valuable reports, which help us to a fair knowledge both of the original features of the institution

and of the attempts made by the British Government from time to time to revive and enforce it.

2. The idea of compulsory labour for the benefit of the Central Government prevailed largely in India under indigenous rule, and continued for some time since the British occupation. It was employed in the construction of temples, palaces, public buildings and roads, and in carrying the baggage of Government officers and other powerful individuals. In a Memorandum on the Administration of India issued in 1858, it was remarked that the last vestige of this practice in a licensed form was in the construction of the Thibet road through the Himalaya Mountains.[1] The great temple of Tanjore in South India, which was erected by the Cholas in the eleventh century A.D., was built largely by forced labour. Tippu Sultan of Mysore (d. 1799) built his fortifications in Seringapatam by carrying off 20,000 labourers from the neighbouring areas, and forcibly keeping them in his employment for years.[2] It is said of the famous South Indian Prince, Tirumala Naick of Madura (d. 1659), that on the occasion of the great festivals at his capital, each village was bound to provide a certain number of men to drag the gigantic cars of the gods in procession, and this service was designated and taxed as *ter-uliyam* or *car service*.[3] The maritime chief Angria (d. 1756), who ruled in Mahrashtra in the middle of the eighteenth century, enforced an elaborate system of taxation by personal service. The low caste tribes, the *Mahars*, were required to serve in the forts one month in the year, and received their subsistence in daily doles of rice from the Government; and certain other castes (the *Kharvees* and the *Daldees*) were bound to supply one man in every eight capable of bearing arms to serve for eight months in the year

[1] *Memorandum on the Administration of India during the Past Thirty Years*, 1858, London, p. 50.

[2] *Memorandum on the Progress of the Madras Presidency during the Last Forty Years*, Srinivāsarāghava Iyengar, 1892, para. 10.

[3] *Calcutta Review*, April 1900. Article: "When Tirumala the Great Ruled."

on board the vessels of war, receiving in return monthly contributions of grain and a small money grant.[1]

3. Compulsory labour in the interests of the village community has been in existence, in some form or other, in nearly every part of India. It has been best developed in its application to irrigation, and it is here that we may study it to the best advantage. A considerable part of the Indian irrigation system consists of small tanks and channels which have been in existence from very remote times, and which were built partly by individual charity and partly by communal enterprise. Two tanks in the Chingleput District of the Madras Presidency have been recognized as finding mention in inscriptions of the eighth and ninth centuries A.D. Epigraphic and literary evidences carry back the existence of irrigation works to still more remote times.[2] It is in the Madras Presidency that irrigation by small tanks and channels is most numerous, where they have been estimated to irrigate "collectively an area equal to that irrigated by all the larger works which have been constructed by the British Government in that Presidency."[3] Whatever the origin of individual works, the duty of maintaining and keeping them in repair was sooner or later recognized by custom to fall upon the village community.

4. On the construction and maintenance of small irrigation works, South Indian inscriptions of the ninth to the twelfth century A.D., recorded in the Madras Epigraphic Reports, throw valuable light. An interesting summary of the facts set out in these inscriptions was contributed to the *Annual Report of the Archæological Survey of India* for 1903–4, by the late Superintendent of Epigraphy, Rai Bahadur V. Venkayya.[4] The

---

[1] *Geographical and Statistical Memoir of the Konkun*, Major T. B. Jarvis, Calcutta, 1840.

[2] *Archæological Survey of India*, 1903–4, pp. 202–11; *The Tamilian Antiquary*, Madras, 1910, pp. 46–8.

[3] *Report of the Indian Irrigation Commission*, 1901–3, part i, p. 8.

[4] Pp. 202–11.

agency by whom tanks and channels were dug or their digging was financed does not appear clearly. Most of the inscriptions deal with the means employed for repairing them and keeping them in order after they were built. But we may assume that the construction of small irrigation works was carried out by the king, by the village assembly, or by private benefactors—oftenest, perhaps, by the last.[1] At any rate it is by these three agencies that the means required for repairing village tanks and channels were supplied; and it is reasonable to suppose that their construction also was due to the same agency. When private persons devoted their charity to beneficent public works, the usual form which it took was a grant of land or of money as an endowment towards their maintenance. The grant was probably administered by the village assembly through one of its committees as a form of public trust. The village temple is frequently mentioned as an accommodating benefactor, and the impression certainly arises on a perusal of early inscriptions that in meeting public needs such as these or great public emergencies like a famine, the temple authorities felt a special sense of responsibility, and often, perhaps, rose to it. The commonest kind of repair which required doing was the removal of accumulated silt. Towards this, provision was made for the supply of boats, of baskets in which to lift the earth, of labourers, of skilled workmen to take care of the boats, and of fishermen to provide certain kinds of necessaries. The village committee which was set to control these operations, we may assume, was the Tank Committee referred to in chapter 1, paragraph 3.

5. The practice of employing communal labour in the repair of village works perhaps arose whenever the

[1] In the erection of bridges in England, it will be remembered that though the erection itself might "be a matter of private or corporate bounty, the law, from the first, took cognizance of its maintenance in repair. When a bridge had once been erected, it became a matter of obvious public convenience that it should be maintained." Webb, *Story of the King's Highway*, p. 86.

means mentioned above failed. If the king's interest in the village waned for any reason or private charity was not forthcoming or the village assembly was short of funds or they had no available waste land with which to endow tanks, it became an obvious necessity to levy a general contribution of labour or wealth. The practice was not confined to tanks and channels, but was employed even in such things as the preparation of a public show or entertainment, the performance of sacrifices, and in other public works like the construction of roads. The *Arthaśāstra* lays down penalties for those who refused to join in or caused obstruction to those who did; and the king's favour was to be shown to any one who loyally did his duty in promoting the requisite forms of communal enterprise.[1]

6. Whatever the origin of the custom of communal labour, it has never been applied, so far as we know, to the initiation of any new works or to repairs of any considerable magnitude. Sir Thomas Munro, who reported on it in 1803, stated that the custom was enforced where the damages to tanks were trifling, "not amounting to above ten, twenty or thirty *pagodas*,"[2] and he did not think the enforcement of it too heavy a burden if the expense of the repairs did not exceed 5 per cent. of the rent of the lands watered by the tank. In a letter addressed by the Madras Government to the Government of India in 1857, they regarded as falling within the operation of the custom such repairs of channels as did not exceed in expense 2½ per cent. of the revenue derived from the village.[3] The Famine Commission of 1880 made the following recommendation as to the limits of works to be repaired by the village community. "Tanks irrigating over 50 acres [and under 200], if found to require repairs, should be brought up to the necessary

[1] *Mysore Review*, August 1908.

[2] A *pagoda* was considered equivalent to Rs. 3½. *Minutes of Sir T. Munro* (Arbuthnot), vol. i, p. 90.

[3] Quoted by the Hon. D. Elliot in the Imperial Legislative Council, April 8, 1857.

standard by the Public Works officers at the cost of the Government, and then handed over to the village officials to be maintained. Those irrigating less than 50 acres should be handed over to village officers, the Department of Public Works doing only masonry work. . . . The smallest class of tanks, irrigating less than 10 acres might be handed over entirely to the ryots. . . ."[1] Usually no payment was made for the labour thus rendered, though occasionally grants in aid were given by the Government for the improvement of specific works.[2] It has been noticed that the custom tends to die out sooner on tanks and rain-fed reservoirs than on water-courses, the reason being that in the latter case the appearance of silt may altogether cut off water supply and destroy the crops, and it is to the self-interest of the cultivator to take prompt action, while in the former case the cultivators may well wait through long years of deterioration till the embankment actually bursts and the water is finally stopped.[3]

7. A detailed description of the manner in which the custom was enforced in regard to works subsidized by the Government in the first half of last century is given in the Report of the Madras Public Works Commission of 1853, from which are taken the following extracts : "As soon as a *Tahsildar* receives orders to execute . . . a work, and has the necessary funds placed at his disposal, he sends to the headman of the village, desiring that they and the *Karnam* (accountant) will come to the *Katcherry* (office), bringing with them workmen to undertake the work. This order is either sent verbally by a *peon* (messenger) or more commonly is a written document. The village may be ten, twenty or even thirty miles distant . . . but in due time the village officers present themselves at the *Katcherry* with the workpeople to undertake the work,

[1] *Report of the Indian Famine Commission*, 1880, part ii, p. 163.
[2] *Ibid.*, App. v, ch. iv, para. 3.
[3] *Report of the Indian Irrigation Commission*, 1901-3, part ii, pp. 110.

and perhaps with a number of the principal ryots or *meerasdars*. The terms of the estimate, viz. the nature of the work to be done, and the rates allowed for doing it, are then explained to the parties, and the terms having been agreed to, written engagements and security bonds are executed, and a portion of the amount of the estimate is advanced. As to the parties of these proceedings, the custom varies in the several districts. In some the workpeople themselves, through their headmen, receive the advance and execute the agreement, while the heads of the village give security for the fulfilment of the terms ; in others the heads of the village receive the advance and execute the agreement, and the principal ryots or *meerasdars* are the sureties. . . . After these preliminaries have been completed, the people return to their village. . . . In the course of time, though generally not without considerable delay, the work is commenced, but it does not advance very rapidly. The advance has been received, but the parties are by no means in a hurry to perform their engagement. . . . The finished works are measured . . . by the *taluk* officers ; the *Karnam* then goes to the *taluk Katcherry* with his accounts . . . and from there in comparison with the estimate and measurement statement the abstract account of the cost is prepared to be sent to the collector. . . . The village *Monigars*, or heads, the people engaged on the work or their headmen, and often the *meerasdars*, or some of them, are sent for, and they sign the accounts which are then despatched to the collector. . . . The people employed are generally under the control of the village officers, and are paid by them at their own convenience, and in money or grain, as they find most to their interest. Complaints to the collector are rare in consequence of the distance, . . . and the labourers are almost entirely at the mercy of the village authorities." [1]

[1] *Second Report of the Commissioners on Public Works in the Madras Presidency*, Madras, 1853, paras. 159, 163, 204. The nearest analogy to this in England

8. The following account of the way in which communal labour is employed to-day unofficially in a Madras district [1] has been gleaned from evidence recorded by a recent Government committee of inquiry. At certain seasons, or on fixed days of the year, the ryots of every village irrigated by the channel in question are expected to contribute labour every day, either by going themselves, or by sending a man, or men, instead. The amount of labour required of each man is measured by the quantity of land held by him in the irrigated area. The whole arrangement is under the supervision of a village officer, appointed by the cultivators themselves. The number of such officers in a village varies from one to sometimes as many as four. They have the right of fining any cultivator who makes default in supplying his quota of labour, the usual rate of fine being four annas each day. A defaulter book is kept, in which all entries with regard to fines are recorded. The amount thus collected is spent usually on some charitable object, such as feeding the poor, but sometimes advantage is taken of it for the construction of a new road in the village. Where a fine is not duly paid or some other breach of rule occurs, the officer refuses to let water on to the land of the defaulter. At no stage of the work is any reference made to a Revenue or Public Works official. [2]

9. Whether under the system of village communal labour the cultivator was obliged to render the necessary service himself, or whether it was open to him to make a grain or cash contribution instead, is a point on which it is difficult to be precise. Sir Thomas Munro, writing in 1803, clearly contemplated an alternative contribution as permissible by custom.

appears to be the obligation which was imposed on parishioners to repair, or provide for the repair, of roads under the supervision of the Surveyor of Highways. Webb, *Story of the King's Highway*, ch. ii.

[1] Anantapur.

[2] Madras Forest Committee, 1913, *Minutes of Evidence*, pp. 423, 428, 438, 439, 453, 463, 471.

According to him the cultivators made the necessary repairs by their own labour, or by an assessment of grain for the payment of professional bricklayers. "There are very few tanks in which ordinary repairs have not always been made, either by the cultivators themselves or by the revenue servants at their expense, by levying a contribution of grain regulated by the quantity of each man's land."[1] When the question was raised by the Public Works Commission (1869–70) as to whether a money cess might be legally imposed instead of enforcing labour, the well-known South Indian administrator, Sir Seshayya Sastry, said: "I am entirely opposed to the commutation of *Kudimaramat*[2] into any form of cess. A cess is no doubt easily collected and as easily squandered away, but what is wanted is that the work be done, and done well, in proper season," and the Hon. Chentsal Rao said: "The ryots would much prefer supplying labour to paying a cess."[3] Although, however, the proposal to impose a legal cess did not meet with approval, the practice of paying a voluntary cess instead of labour had been steadily growing, and grain gradually gave way to cash in the payment of the cess. The money so collected is spent by the revenue officials in executing repairs which would otherwise be effected by customary labour.[4] The tendency to substitute a voluntary cess has been specially noticeable in regard to channels which supply water to a number of different villages, in which case the machinery of communal labour would be more difficult to employ. It is so clearly to the interest of the villagers to promptly pay the cess that the want of a legal sanction has not been felt as a distinct weakness. The Irrigation Commission (1901–3), while prepared to recommend a statutory

[1] *Minutes of Sir T. Munro* (Arbuthnot), vol. i, p. 90.

[2] Communal labour.

[3] Quoted by Col. R. H. Sankey, R.E., in Madras Legislative Council, June 18, 1883.

[4] *Imperial Gazetteer of India*, vol. xvi, p. 279.

money cess in certain cases, recommended that for the administration of the cess there should be constituted local *panchayats*, "the object being to get the people themselves to feel a proprietary interest and pride in their tank."[1]

10. The constitution of a separate Department of Public Works took place in Madras in 1856-7. It took charge, among other things, of the repairs of irrigation works which had till then formed part of the duties of the collector and his subordinates. But the new Public Works Department lacked the executive and magisterial powers of the collector and his staff, and consequently their authority over the villagers in enforcing the obligation of customary labour speedily waned. It was therefore felt necessary, if the right was not to be lost to the Government, to seek the aid of the Legislature, and an Act was passed by the Legislative Council of the Governor-General in 1858, the *Madras Compulsory Labour Act* giving the requisite legal sanction. The Act laid down the following rule: "Whenever it shall appear to the officer in charge of any tank, river, or canal or other like works, that there is any imminent danger of the embankment of such tank, etc., being breached, which may be prevented by a large body of labourers immediately working together, it shall be lawful for such officer to require the head of the village in the vicinity to call upon all able-bodied male persons of the labouring classes in such village to co-operate in the work."[2] The Act, however, has remained practically inoperative. The causes of this failure were set out by Sir A. T. Arundel in a pamphlet which he published on communal labour in 1879.[3] The main cause was the insufficient wording of the Act, which sanctions the

[1] *Report of the Indian Irrigation Commission*, 1901-3, part ii, p. 114.

[2] Sec. 1.

[3] *Irrigation and Communal Labour in the Madras Presidency*, A. T. Arundel, I.C.S., Madras, 1879, ch. iv.

powers given under it, only in cases where the custom may be proved to be actually incumbent on the local village community, and it has been found to be no light matter, in the midst of a continual disintegration of the old village community, to establish the continuance of the custom in a court of law in any particular case. Another cause was that legal proceedings under the Act had to be taken "against each separate defaulter, on each separate occasion, and practically on the motion of village officers"—a ruling which rendered the procedure exceedingly lethargic.

11. It is clear from the testimony of successive commissions of inquiry that the institution of communal labour has not altogether died out in the Madras Presidency. The Public Works Commission of 1869–70 went minutely into the question, and produced a large mass of evidence to prove its continuance. All the witnesses said, practically without a dissentient voice, that whether the labour was exacted or spontaneously contributed, the custom prevailed, more or less, in every part of the Presidency. The annual value of the unpaid labour utilized in various districts was estimated in Trichinopoly at Rs. 50,000, in North Arcot at Rs. 60,000, and in Tanjore at Rs. 300,000.[1] The Famine Commission of 1880, through their special Committee on Irrigation, reported that so far as the irrigation by small spring channels was concerned, "it is still generally performed by the free labour of the ryot."[2] On the report of this Commission and the results of previous inquiries, a bill for legalizing the custom was introduced in the Madras Legislative Council in 1883, but was eventually dropped. The Indian Irrigation Commission (1901–3) said: "We were repeatedly assured that the maintenance of the tanks was not satisfactory, and that *Kudimaramat* was practically dead. Others regarded

[1] Pamphlet by Mr. Arundel, ch. iv.

[2] *Report of the Indian Famine Commission*, 1880, App. v, ch. iv, para. 5.

it as only moribund. . . . We are ourselves reluctant to admit that so valuable an institution is really dead and past restoration."[1] Further testimony on the point was recorded by the Madras Forest Committee (1913), who brought out a very interesting collection of facts on the communal system of irrigation still prevalent in what are known as the Ceded Districts.

12. The capital required for the construction of public works in a village is usually contributed, in accordance possibly with ancient usage, by wealthy individuals to whom such works appeal as an attractive form of charitable endowment. But there has also been a considerable amount of communal effort by the village as a whole in raising capital, and that it is even now shown in various spheres of village life is a proof that the old corporate life of the village is not a thing of the past. We have seen it already in the erection of school buildings and of famine works. The more common method of raising the capital required for a work undertaken jointly by the community is by levying voluntary subscriptions. Sir A. T. Arundel, writing about Madras in 1879, said: "During the settlement of the Tinnevelly District more than Rs. 250,000 were raised by subscription and by the sale of waste land, and expended upon objects of public utility, chiefly irrigation works. On one channel alone the ryots built forty-six substantial masonry sluices. . . . In another village Rs. 1,000 was subscribed by the ryots, and expended in clearing away accumulations of silt from neglected public channels. Four villages united to subscribe Rs. 2,500 to build regulating works to apportion the water supply. . . . Indeed so numerous were the applications from village communities desirous of raising subscriptions for works of public utility in which they were individually interested, that the authorities were unable to pay

[1] *Report*, part ii, p. 112.

attention to them all."[1] In a speech which he made in the Bombay Legislative Council in 1889 on the subject of voluntary contributions under the Village Sanitation Act, Sir Raymond West remarked: "It is said that it is impossible to get subscriptions. . . . I do not think so. . . . The practice prevails in this Presidency, with which as a District Officer I was once personally familiar, and I find that in one *taluka* sixteen villages in the course of two years have subscribed a considerable sum for building and making tanks in their villages."[2] Besides voluntary subscriptions, it used to be the practice for village communities in the Deccan to raise the necessary capital by a public loan. This was resorted to in cases where the expense was too great for the village to defray at once. The debt was gradually redeemed by an annual assessment, and sometimes by mortgages of grants of land on the part of the villagers. If the grant of land was small, no rent was charged by Government, but if it was a large grant, the revenue was paid by the other ryots, and the creditor still enjoyed the land rent-free.[3]

13. We have been speaking so far of the presence of communal labour in the Madras Presidency. The system was best developed in the Southern Province, but it exists also in some measure in other parts of India, and a rapid survey may he made of the important areas where it is still found. In Gujarat in the Bombay Presidency, though not so pronounced as in Madras, it still exists, and the Irrigation Commission (1901–3) strongly recommended its revival.[4] In Nasik (Bombay) the *Bhandharas* (i.e. weirs constructed for raising the level of flowing water across rivers) are erected by the Government, but their recurrent repairs

[1] Pamphlet by Mr. Arundel, p. 45.
[2] Bombay Legislative Council, September 7, 1889.
[3] *Report on the Territories Conquered from the Paishwa*, Ephinstone, p. 26.
[4] *Report of the Indian Irrigation Commission*, 1901–3, part ii, p. 51.

and cleaning are left in the hands of the villagers.[1] The *Vaderu* in Sind (an ancient village officer) had, till about forty years ago, the duty of summoning the villagers for the annual clearance of the canals and water-courses.[2] In the Bhandhara District in the Central Provinces the village record-of-rights (*Wajib-ul-arz*) lays down the duty of the cultivators to do all the minor repairs, and of the village landlord (*Malguzar*) to do the greater repairs.[3] A similar provision is entered in the village records of the Santal Parganas in Bengal, declaring it the duty of the headman and ryots of a village to maintain and repair all the village tanks and other works of irrigation.[4] In Bhagalpur (Bengal) the responsibility for the maintenance of the *Janghas*, or small canals, is left with the ryots of the village.[5] In the Punjab in the Kangra Valley the cuts from the hill streams called *Kuls* are managed by the people themselves, with no assistance from the Government. "They maintain an organized staff of officers, every village supplying its representatives, who patrol the water-courses to prevent theft, to stop leakages and to distribute the water."[6] In the Zhob District in Baluchistan the old type of irrigation wells called *Karezes* is undertaken by joint capital divided among several co-sharers, whose shares are determined by the amount of water consumed by each. The work is carried out under the supervision of the *Mirab*, or headman, the co-partners themselves providing labour in works which require no special skill.[7] In the North-West Frontier Province in Bannu canal clearance is carried out by unpaid labour called *tinga*, and the fines imposed upon defaulters constitute what is

1 Evidence of A. H. A. Simcox, I.C.S., before the Irrigation Commission, 1901–3.
2 *Bombay Gazette*, 1881, part v, p. 24.
3 Evidence of A. B. Napier, I.C.S., before Irrigation Commission, 1901–3.
4 *Bengal District Gazetteers*, Santal Parganas, pp. 161–2.
5 *Ibid*., Bhagalpur, p. 83.
6 *Punjab District Gazetteers*, Kangra, pp. 144–5.
7 *Baluchistan District Gazetteers*, Zhob, pp. 150–4.

called the *Nagha* fund at the disposal of the Deputy Commissioner.[1]

14. There is an extensive system of irrigation by means of small canals in Upper Burma with a complete organization for communal management. "The canals are managed by those who own land irrigated by them, who are also responsible for the necessary labour. On each canal there is a *Myaung-gaung*, or headman, and one or two criers. These officials are elected from their number by those interested in the canal, who are called *Myaung-thas*. The *gaung* allots tasks to the *Myaung-thas*, which are proportioned to the area of land to be irrigated possessed by each. On each canal there is a unit of measure of land, called a *det*, and a unit of measure of work, called a *ta*. These vary in each system. The *det* may be an area of land estimated to produce a certain outturn of paddy, or estimated to require a certain number of bundles of seedlings or of baskets of seed for its cultivation. Situation and quality of the land to be irrigated are taken into account, so that the actual area of a *det* on a single system is not necessarily uniform. For each *det* one labourer is required, for the supply of whom the owner or owners of the land included in the *det* are responsible. Either an owner may personally labour or the labourers required may be furnished by the *gaung* on payment of a fixed sum. In the case of a *det* owned by more than one man (and such ownership is common) the co-owners arrange among themselves for the provision of labour or for payment in its stead. Though theoretically one labourer is required for each *det*, in practice the number of owners who actually perform personal labour is usually sufficient for the work to be done, and these share among them the payments made for substitutes. The *gaung* and criers do no actual labour, their duties being

[1] *North-West Frontier Province District Gazetteers*, Bannu, pp. 94–5.

confined to supervision. The criers communicate the orders of the *gaung* to the *Myaung-thas* and call them out in case of breaches. . . . Each *Myaung-tha* is responsible for the minor channels which actually lead the water from the canal into his fields." [1]

15. The actual distribution of water in an irrigated village from the main outlet into each field is very often left to the arrangement of the cultivators themselves. There is sometimes a *panchayat* appointed by the cultivators to regulate the water-supply, but more often a single village officer. This office is an ancient institution, remunerated even to this day in some parts of the country by grain fees contributed by the cultivators,[2] and its holder works under the immediate orders of the headman. In the large majority of villages at present there is no organization of any kind for the distribution of water within the village. It is carried out, for aught we know, in a haphazard way. There are some villages, however, which possess a regular system of time-honoured rules for distributing water. The following system which prevails in the Zhob District (Baluchistan) is devised with great ingenuity. "A dial is made of a straight stick, twelve fingers high, which is planted in level ground at sunrise. Subsequent operations are explained by the following diagram :—

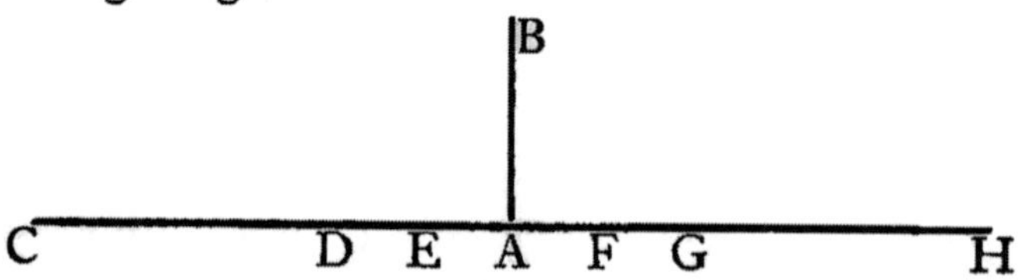

AB represents the stick and CH the groundline, the first *atama* [3] after sunrise is considered to be over when the shadow of the stick has receded to the point C,

[1] *Burma District Gazetteers*, Pakokku, pp. 46–7.

[2] Evidence of C. H. Mounsey, I.C.S. (Madras), and R. S. Baitmangalkar, Deputy Collector (Bombay), before Irrigation Commission, 1901–3.

[3] Eighth part of the day.

which is twenty-four fingers' breadth distant from the point A. The second *atama* is over when the shadow has moved twelve fingers further and is at D, while each of the two subsequent *atamas* up to mid-day are represented by a movement for the breadth of six fingers each. In the afternoon the reverse process is followed, the last *atama* lasting from the time the shadow has reached the point H till sunset." [1] In discussing the nature of the rules by which a village community regulated its water-supply, Sir Henry Maine expressed the opinion that they rested for their sanction neither upon the personal authority of the author nor on a sense of equity nor on any express or implied agreement, but rather upon a sort of fiction which represented them to have existed from all antiquity.[2]

16. A word must be said of the form of compulsory labour known as *Begar*, which prevails in villages in Upper India. Two varieties of this may be noticed—one enforced by the Government, and the other by the village landlord. The former existed in practically an unimpaired form in certain parts of the Punjab till recently, having been abolished in Kangra proper only in 1884 and in Kulu in 1896, and apparently still exists in the hill district of Simla.[3] It was a service which all those who cultivated the soil were bound to render to the Government as a condition of their tenure. It involved generally three different duties—viz. to carry loads, to convey messages or letters, and to provide wood and grass for camp. The amount of labour required was calculated rather on each individual cultivator than on each homestead. The order for the abolition of Government *Begar* in the Punjab does not extend, however, to labour for which full payment is made, and landowners are still expected to turn out for

[1] *Baluchistan District Gazetteers*, Zhob, pp. 15c–4.
[2] *Village Communities in the East and the West*, Lecture iv.
[3] *Punjab District Gazetteers*, Simla, p. 106.

such labour under certain conditions.[1] The other form of *Begar*, viz. that exacted by the landlord, is still found in various parts of Upper India. It generally takes the form of labour on the landlord's fields for a stated number of days in the year, to be fixed with reference to each successive harvest. The cultivator is also bound to provide the landlord with a plough and sometimes a bullock for a day at each harvest. In some places they have also to help in thatching the landlord's house, and sometimes to give him their labour free when there is a marriage in his family, or he goes on a journey. The village artisans, not seldom, are also bound similarly to work for the landlord when needed.[2]

17. The chief public buildings usually found in a village are the meeting-house which is often no more than an open shed, a guest-house, a temple or mosque, a school where such exists, and the relics of the old tower where the inhabitants used to store their property on the occasion of a sudden raid. Often these buildings are found merged in one another, and there is no clear demarcation of the uses to which they may be put in the exigencies of village life. It is difficult to trace any regular system on which they are built or repaired, but it is safe to assume that private charity and communal labour entered into the construction and maintenance of these buildings as well as of village roads and communications in the same manner, though not perhaps to the same extent, as into irrigation works. The maintenance of roads and communications is at present largely the responsibility of District and Local Boards, but the obligation of the village community to look after them is still definitely recognized in some parts of the country. An instance

[1] *Punjab District Gazetteers*, Kangra, pp. 186–8.

[2] *Bengal District Gazetteers*, Palamau, pp. 134–5; *Central Provinces and Berar District Gazetteers*, Bhandhara, p. 159. Compare the services rendered by a tenant to his manorial lord in England, Vinogradoff, *Growth of the Manor*, pp. 327–8.

of it is the small village paths in Almora (United Provinces), for the maintenance of which engagements are still made with village landlords at the time of the land settlement.[1] So in Burma in the Lower Chindwin District, rural foot-tracts are still the recognized charge of the village community. In 1905–6 the total length of such tracks for which the villagers undertook responsibility was estimated to have been 384 miles.[2]

18. A somewhat unique experiment has been recently tried in Berhampore in the Madras Presidency in the direction of starting village *panchayats* to take control of public works. It is apparently nothing more than an informal measure adopted on the initiative of an individual officer of Government. The principle of the scheme is to divide the villages situated in a sub-division of a district, for the purpose of the scheme, among the members of the Local Board in charge of the sub-division. Each member is set to supervise a small definite group of villages. It is his duty in each of the villages, by instructing the villagers and co-operating with them, to get them to form *panchayats* for supervising works of public utility in the village. A certain sum of money is deposited with each *panchayat* for necessary expenses. When the money is spent or nearly spent, a report is made to the Local Board member, who is in charge of the particular village, and he makes a further advance. Such advances are to be made by the member only after he has satisfied himself of the progress which has been already made. It is too soon to say what will come of the experiment. But a recent report which appeared in an influential Madras newspaper seems to give ground for hope. According to it, the *panchayats* are "so keen and trustworthy that it is a matter of pride with them to do the work."[3]

[1] *United Provinces District Gazetteers*, Almora, p. 110.
[2] *Burma District Gazetteers*, Lower Chindwin, p. 141.
[3] The *Hindu*, weekly edition, April 8, 1915, p. 2.

CHAPTER VI

WATCH AND WARD

1. In the ancient village community, the headman had the principal direction of the arrangements for watch and ward. His chief executive assistant was the village watchman, who stood to him practically in the relation of a personal servant. As a rule, he was one of the menial castes, often given to criminal habits, who lived on the outskirts of the village and performed general service for the community His position in the village has been noticed in a previous chapter in connection with the sanitary duties which he discharged in addition to his police functions. He was responsible, under the supervision of the headman, not merely for the discovery of lost property, but for replacing its value when not discovered. In the joint landholding communities of Upper India, the police responsibility of the single headman was divided among the landowners who, between them, maintained order in the village, and through their servants restored, or replaced the value of, lost property. The village communities were everywhere held jointly responsible for offences committed within their limits,[1] and any penalties awarded in consequence were liable to mutual apportionment. When necessity arose, the watchman was assisted by the members of his family, by the other village servants, and in some cases by the whole village com-

[1] Compare the joint responsibility for crime of a township in England in later Saxon times. Vinogradoff, *The Growth of the Manor*, pp. 196–9.

munity.[1] Such a necessity arose whenever a serious theft occurred in the village. It was then customary for the watchman, assisted by the general body of villagers, to start in pursuit of the thief, and the search was only given up when the offender had been definitely traced to an adjacent village, when the responsibility was understood to shift to the members of that village.[2]

2. One of the most graphic accounts that we have of the duties performed by the village watchman under former governments is that given by Elphinstone of the watchman in the Maratha country.[3] The description is worth quoting. "The duties are to keep watch at night, to find out all arrivals and departures, observe all strangers and report all suspicious persons to the *Patel*. The watchman is likewise bound to know the character of each man in the village, and in the event of a theft committed within the village bounds, it is his business to detect the thief. He is enabled to do this by his early habits of inquisitiveness and observation as well as by the nature of his allowance, which being partly a small share of the grain and similar property belonging to each house, he is kept always on the watch to ascertain his fees and always in motion to collect them. When a theft or robbery happens, the watchman commences his inquiries and researches; it is very common for him to track a thief by his footsteps; and if he does this to another village so as to satisfy the watchman there, or if he otherwise traces the property to an adjoining village, his responsibility ends." The remuneration of the village police took the usual form of grain-fees, occasional perquisites, and endowments of land. A Commission appointed in 1858 to deal with ancient grants of land for public purposes in the Madras Presidency men-

1 *Report of the Indian Police Commission* (1902–3), para. 8.
2 This really amounts to raising a "hue and cry."
3 *Report on the Territories Conquered from the Paishwa*, Elphinstone, p. 47.

tioned nine cases of such grants, among which were included the following two: (1) grants connected with the general police of the country under former rulers, and (2) grants to village headmen, accountants, and village police.[1] With regard to the responsibility of the watchman to make good lost property, Elphinstone's remark may be noted that his obligation was limited by the extent of his means, while the remainder was levied on the village as a whole, and that it was only in particular cases that this indemnity was enforced at all. Where indemnity was directed to be paid and the headman or watchman refused, the punishment was the transfer of the assigned land to the nearest relation, fine, imprisonment in irons or severe corporal punishment.[2]

3. The exact manner in which the village police was linked up with the Central Government is not easy to trace, but it may be presumed that it was in some such way as this: The village police, with the headman and the watchman, were looked upon as the immediate working agency. Over them, in many cases, were officers set in charge of groups of villages, assisted by armed followers, who, in respect of this wider area, had much the same duties and obligations as the village police in the village. Over these again, not infrequently, were officers in charge of districts, and over them the governor of the province.[3] This, of course, is a very rough and perhaps hypothetical description, and applicable only to limited areas and to comparatively recent times. The intermediate officers between the village and the provincial Government were known as *Kavalgars* and *Palegars* in parts of the Madras Presidency—names around which have gathered bitter tales of pillage and plunder. To the

[1] *Land Systems of British India*, Baden Powell, vol. iii, p. 78.
[2] *Report on the Territories Conquered from the Paishwa*, Elphinstone, p. 47.
[3] *Papers Connected with the Reorganization of the Police in the Madras Presidency*, 1859, pp. 43–5.

same class belonged in Telingana or the old Telugu country the police official called *Munewar*. Sir Richard Temple wrote of him in 1868: "The Munewar's original function was to supervise the village watch and to keep the peace generally within a certain circle of villages. For this work he received either allowances drawn from the land or a landed grant. At first these men were doubtless hereditary police officers. In later days they often figure as rural chiefs, and sometimes either as turbulent subjects or as persons resolute to resist aggression, whether from government or from their neighbours."[1] Under this class of connecting links with the central Government may be mentioned also the detective police inspectors known as *Tapasnavis*, appointed by the famous Maratha administrator, Nana Farnavis (d. 1800).[2]

4. We have an interesting account in the *Fifth Report* (1812)[3] of the financial arrangements connected with the institution of *Palegars*, the old police chieftains of the Madras Presidency, as it obtained during the troublous times which immediately preceded the British occupation. They fulfilled two capacities—first as district watchers, and secondly as village watchers. And corresponding to these two functions, they collected two kinds of fees—the village watching fee called *Stallum Kaval*, and the district watching fee called *Desha Kaval*. The former was really the police contributions of the village community meant to support the village watchmen, but the *Palegars* had so encroached on the position of the watchman that, in order to appropriate the fees due to them, their retainers undertook to discharge the duties of the watchmen and practically drove them in large numbers out of occupation. In the district of Tinnevelly, with its 2,000 villages, there were in 1799 only 477 with watchmen of the

[1] *Report on the Administration of the Government of H.H. the Nizam*, R. Temple, Calcutta, 1868, para. 143.

[2] *Imperial Gazetteer of India*, vol. viii, p. 370.

[3] P. 142.

ancient communal type; and even these were allowed to retain their places only on condition of contributing a share of the emoluments attached to the office. The district watching fee was often the gift of the king; but sometimes it was the gift of defenceless villagers, who paid it partly to guard against roving bands of plunderers and partly to prevent the *Palegars* themselves from plundering them. The Report goes on to say: "These contributions consisted in payments in money, grain, ploughs, or cattle, and various other articles, and were raised by armed peons. They were not regulated by any fixed principle, but the amount depended on the conscience of the *Palegar*. The payment was sometimes enforced by torture and the whip, and the whole village was put into confinement and every occupation interdicted."

5. The practice by which defenceless villagers were led to engage the services of plundering robber chieftains to secure them against robbery and violence, was part of an extensive system of what might be called "private police." The system must have prevailed in most parts of the country during the political upheaval of the seventeenth and eighteenth centuries. The *Palegars* of South India were in reality not different in their methods, and the causes which gave them birth, from the Marathas in Western India, or from the *Pindaris* and the *Thugs*, all of whom were characteristic products of a time which witnessed a universal breakdown of governments and dynasties. There is evidence that this practice of employing men privately for police purposes goes back to ancient times. The *Arthas'āstra* mentions wild tribes (*Aranyachara*) among those who may be used to protect the interior of the kingdom.[1] A South Indian inscription of the fourteenth century A.D., represents a village assembly as selling the right of *Padikkaval*, that is, possibly, the

[1] *Mysore Review*, February 1907.

right of guarding the village.[1] The essence of the system was that the inhabitants of a village entered into a formal contract with the head of a neighbouring tribe of marauders by which, in return for a specified payment, he agreed to protect them against invasion and robbery, and in case of theft to compensate them for the loss. Very often the real objective of this precaution was the contracting tribe themselves—it was a payment they expected "for kindly desisting from robbery."[2] The practice has survived to this day, in some form or other, in spite of systematic efforts to put it down. In the Madras Presidency the two criminal tribes who are prominently associated with this custom are the *Kallars* and the *Maravars* in the Madura, Tinnevelly, and adjoining districts, and the institution is called *Tuppu-Kuli* and *Kudikaval.* In the United Provinces[3] the *Gujars* and the *Jats*, and in Bombay[4] the *Ramosis* are the tribes employed for purposes of private police, and the system in the former province is called *Languri.* Corresponding to these in Burma[5] is the system of cases known as *Pyan-pe*, and in the Punjab[6] the cash gratifications known as *Bunga.* There is nothing to show that the contract is not, as a rule, faithfully discharged by the tribes concerned, and indeed it often happens that a village finds it a more satisfactory method of safeguarding its property, the ways of the regular police being formal and sometimes harassing. Speaking broadly, then, it may be said that the police arrangements of the village before British rule began consisted of the village watch and the private police or the village guard. The former were concerned with offences within the village, the latter with offences from without.

1 *Madras Epigraphy*, *Annual Report*, 1908–9, pp. 82–3.
2 *Thillai Govindan*, Madras, p. 2.
3 *United Provinces Police Report*, 1906, para. 120.
4 *Police and Crime in India*, Sir E. Cox, London, ch. iii.
5 *Burma District Gazetteers*, Thayetmyo, vol. A, p. 49.
6 *Punjab Police Report*, 1903, para. 17.

6. It may be of interest to set out a few facts regarding the "private police" system, especially in the Madras Presidency, and of the efforts made to put it down. It is the history of a movement which began as a real necessity during a time of general lawlessness, as the only method of safeguarding life and property; but the vested interests it has created by providing through centuries a lucrative occupation for whole tribes of men, combined with the sense of necessity and fear which the traditions of former disorders have helped to sustain, has turned the movement into a grave standing abuse, against which, in the new regime of law and order, the resources of Government have had to be employed with unceasing vigilance. The foremost of these tribes in the South, called the *Kallars*,[1] have a history which apparently goes back for many centuries. Mr. Vincent Smith has suggested the possibility that the *Kallars* are the same race as the *Pallavas*, who exercised such great political dominion in South India in the centuries previous to the Muhammadan invasions, and that the "bold predatory habits" which the *Kallars* display correspond, from what we know, to the manner in which the *Pallavas* exercised their power.[2] He also notes that during the first three centuries of the Christian Era, the frequent wars which occurred among the various independent chieftains of South India were often waged by the agency of these aboriginal tribesmen.[3] The methods employed by them of plundering and of levying tribute were not different from those adopted by the Marathas several centuries later, in connection with their levy of the famous tribute known as *Chauth*. Indeed there is evidence that when the Marathas ventured into the extreme South they enlisted the

---

[1] An excellent account of the *Kallars* will be found in *Yusuf Khan, the Rebel Commandant*, by S. C. Hill (Longmans, 1914), pp. 25–6.

[2] *Early History of India*, V. A. Smith, Oxford, 1914, p. 470.

[3] *Ibid.*, pp. 439–40.

co-operation of the *Kallars*. When, for example, the Maratha General Raghoji Bhonsla attacked Trichinopoly, among the forces which he led were numbered the *Kallars* besides other tribes.[1] A splendid opportunity for the exercise of their time-honoured profession came to them when Haidar Ali of Mysore made his invasion of 1781 and in the wide-spread disorder which followed it. We find, therefore, that the movement which the Madras police are still engaged in fighting, has to be traced to habits whose roots lie away back in the dim ages of antiquity.

7. The agreement by which the inhabitants of a village engage the services of a criminal tribe often consists of two parts—one which is preventive, that is, engaging the tribe to protect them against future offences—and the other which deals with restoration or compensation in regard to offences which have already occurred—a combination, in fact, of police and insurance. In Madras the term *Kudikaval* (joint watch) is ordinarily applied to the first, and the term *Tuppu-Kuli* (clue-hire) to the second. It is not clear whether the system as found in the other provinces has a preventive side to it, or is merely concerned with the restoration of stolen things or replacement of their value. It is not unusual in either case to find the agreement executed with a fair show of legal formalities, such as witnesses and written documents ; and cases sometimes occur of suits being filed in courts of law for the due fulfilment of the contract. The actual parties to the transaction do not, as a rule, come face to face, but leave themselves to be represented by agents. Cattle thefts are the most usual form of offences with which the system is found connected,[2] partly because

---

[1] *The Private Diary of Anandaranga Pillay*, Madras, vol. i, p. 161.

[2] Judging by the provisions about it in Anglo-Saxon law, theft, especially of cattle and horses, appears to have been by far the commonest and most troublesome of offences then. Pollock & Maitland, *History of English Law*, vol. i, pp. 55–6.

cattle form the most valuable property of the agriculturist next to land, and partly because of their mobility. In Tanjore the fee levied is generally from 4 to 8 annas and sometimes 1 rupee per annum for a pair of bulls.[1] These fees must be considered moderate. Indeed it is a point of strength with these robber guards, that they seldom drive the people to desperation by enormous demands. The penalty with which a villager is visited who proves recalcitrant is a surreptitious loot of his things, in the course of which he finds "his standing crops taken from his field, his straw-stack or house on fire, or his best pair of bullocks missing."[2]

8. It is a remarkable fact that after all these years during which this system of blackmail has gone on, there has been but little conscious effort on the part of the people to co-operate in suppressing it. This may be traced to various causes—to fear of vengeance, to long continued habit, to the convenience of avoiding formal police investigations and judicial inquiries, and certainly also to the moderation and discretion of the tribesmen themselves. The only instance of their acting so as to provoke the enmity of the villagers happened in the Madura District in 1896–7 when, owing to certain unprecedented exactions, a general revolt took place which resulted in serious riots. "Meetings of villagers were held, at which thousands attended; they took oath on their ploughs to dispense with the services of the *Kallars*; they formed funds to compensate such of them as lost their cattle or whose houses were burnt; they arranged for watchmen among themselves to patrol the villages at night; they provided horns to be sounded to carry the alarm in case of thefts from village to village, and they prescribed a regular scale of fines to be paid by those villagers who failed to turn out on the sound of the

[1] *Madras District Gazetteers*, Tanjore, pp. 205–6.
[2] *Ibid.*, Madura, pp. 90–3.

alarm."[1] But the agitation begun so well led in the end to no permanent result; and whatever improvement has occurred in recent years has been mainly due to the activities of the regular police and little to any change in public opinion. The chiet measures adopted so far have been to organize special police parties for collecting information, to demand sufficient security from leaders of criminal gangs, to effect a system of registration of cattle sales, so as to prevent questionable transactions and to insist on branding cattle for easy discovery in case of theft.[2] The only really satisfactory means, however, would be the reformation of the tribesmen themselves—and attempts towards this have recently been made by putting them to the more genteel but less exciting profession of rice cultivation,[3] and by the formation among them of co-operative credit societies.

9. While the system of private police, inherited from a time of anarchy and disorder now long past, has thus become a veritable hindrance to good government, its counterpart, the ancient village watch, which maintained internal order in the village, has been on the whole an object of solicitude to the British Government from as far back as the beginning of last century. Lord Hastings, as Governor-General, described them in 1815 as "the foundation of all possible police in this country," and declared that "upon their renovation, improvement, and stability depends the ultimate success of all our measures for the benefit of the country in the prevention, detection, and punishment of crime."[4] Sir Thomas Munro, in a Minute written in 1824, protested strongly against the idea of absorbing the village watch into the regular police system, "for no system for any part of the

[1] *Madras Police Report*, 1896–7, para. 5.
[2] *Ibid.*, 1906–7, para. 21, and 1910–1, para 22.
[3] *Madras District Gazetteers*, Madura, pp. 90–3.
[4] Quoted in the Bengal Legislative Council by A. Money, C.B., May 21, 1870.

municipal administration can ever answer that is not drawn from its ancient institutions or assimilated with them."[1] The experience of provincial governments in regard to the usefulness of the system, in spite of its varying fortunes, was expressed in the *Bombay Administration Report* of 1882–3 in these words: "The actual importance of the village police cannot for a moment be overlooked. Without the aid of the village police not a single offence could be traced out. They are the real backbone of the detective police, they know all that is going on and know every one in the villages."[2] Sir Andrew Fraser's Police Commission (1902–3) went quite as far as any previous authority in declaring the necessity of maintaining the village watch. "This is necessary from the purely Government point of view—it is impossible to support the expense of a force which would be adequate to obtain information regarding crime over the extensive area and among the vast population of India, without securing the co-operation and enforcing the responsibility of the village authorities. It is necessary also from the people's point of view; even if the expensive establishment required could be maintained, it would be vexatious and intolerable to the people. Constant interference by the police, constant espionage on village life, constant visits of officials of the lowest grades constitute an intolerable burden to the people."[3]

10. The history of the reorganization of the village police in Bengal affords an excellent illustration of the strenuous but shifting policy by which Government attempted to materialize their intentions in regard to this problem, as it is also an example of the peculiar difficulties connected with it. The year 1870 may be taken as the chief landmark in this history. It saw the passing of the most important legislative enactment on

[1] *Minute on the State of the Country and Condition of the People in Fort St. George*, 1824.

[2] P. 24.

[3] *Report*, ch. iii.

village police, the *Bengal Chaukidari Act.*[1] It may, therefore, be convenient to divide the story into three parts with reference to this year 1870 : first, the attempts made before the passing of the Act ; second, the provisions of the Act ; and third, the amendments effected subsequently.

11. In Bengal, as in most parts of India, the watchman was originally an officer of the village community, paid by, and responsible to, the community. A great change, however, came over their position during the period of Mughal rule. The Mughal Government was, above all, a fiscal government, and on their fiscal agents, the zemindars, they conferred powers which practically left in their hands many of the instruments of administration. The village watchmen became their personal servants, looking after their affairs by day and watching the village by night. Their functions grew more fiscal than police—more the collection of public dues than the maintenance of order. Under Clive's arrangement in 1765, the Company became possessed of the revenues of Bengal, and the village watchmen, in their new capacity of revenue officers, passed under the control of the Company.[2] The system still suffered from their personal allegiance as a class to the zemindars, and all early efforts at reform failed signally. The Permanent Settlement of Lord Cornwallis in 1793 offered an opportunity for reconsidering the whole position of the zemindars, and it was used to deprive them of their control over the village watchmen, who were transferred to the jurisdiction of the Government police inspectors known as *darogahs*. This meant, in theory at any rate, that they were thereafter to be under the jurisdiction of the regular police. The change, however, was only nominal, as the zemindars, by their enormous local influence, now strengthened by the new proprietary

[1] Act vi. (B.C.) of 1870.

[2] *The Annals of Rural Bengal*, W. W. Hunter, 1868, p. 333.

right under the Permanent Settlement, continued to retain their control over the village watch, and used it to pervert the course of justice in their own interests. The position of the watchman was thus made vague and indeterminate. He was, by law, under the regular police; he was, in practice, the zemindar's man. In either case there was now no question of responsibility to the village community, the dominant position of the zemindar under the Mughals, now sealed by the Permanent Settlement, having thrown the community into comparative powerlessness. This was practically the position of the village police in Bengal until 1870.

12. It must be pointed out that there are considerable parts of Bengal, especially Eastern Bengal, where the village watchmen, as they are found to-day, are not the survivals of the ancient system, but purely a modern creation. In the reports of district officers in those parts of Bengal during the early years of last century, there is evidence that they found little signs of a village police, and some of them on their own account instituted a rural police service corresponding to what obtained in other parts. In fact, the oldest legislative enactment (1817) now in force in Bengal[1] to formulate the position of village watchmen was passed primarily with a view to vindicating the independent action of these district officers.[2] An important test for distinguishing the two systems, the survival of the old from the new artificial creation, was found in the fact that the remuneration of the watchmen under the former system was to a considerable extent derived from assignments of land, while under the latter it was entirely payment by money. This led to the further difference that a watchman who held land in a zemindar's estate was bound, at least by long usage, to render personal service to him in addition to discharging his public duties, while in the other case

[1] Reg. xx. of 1817.

[2] Speech by the Hon. H. J. S. Cotton, Bengal Legislative Council, July 30, 1892.

his responsibility was rather to the general body of villagers under the direction of the magistrate. He owed his maintenance to contributions by the villagers, and his appointment to the magistrate on the nomination of the headman. The main defect with this latter class was that the wages paid to them were often very inadequate and were constantly in arrears. The question whether a zemindar was entitled to the personal service of a watchman who held land in his estate was the subject of a long dispute in Bengal, which was ultimately carried to the Privy Council. The decision of the Privy Council was a compromise to the effect that the watchman's service was partly public service and partly personal service to the zemindar.[1]

13. A strong movement to remedy the accumulated confusion which marked the position of the village police in Bengal started from the great reforms in criminal administration which took place in 1862.[2] In that year were introduced the Indian Penal Code, the Criminal Procedure Code, and the Police Act, and in that year also the High Court took the place of the older courts—the Supreme Court and the *Sadr Nizamat Adalat*.[3] The effect of these changes was to make a great demand for efficiency on the regular police and the magistracy, which was bound to have its influence on the village police, upon whom the first duties in connection with the detection of offences often rested. Various unsuccessful attempts were made at reform. The first of them, which was made sometime before 1862, was the work of Sir H. Ricketts, who brought forward a Bill in 1859 for the formation of a *panchayat* to assess and collect the salaries of the watchmen, but leaving their appointment and removal to the magistrate. This was followed in 1863 by the proposal of Sir Charles Hobhouse to do away with payment by

[1] Joykissen Mookherjee's Case.

[2] *Report of the Committee to Consider the Reform of the Police of the Lower Provinces of Bengal*, Calcutta, 1891.

[3] Principal Criminal Court.

lands and grain-fees, and to make the watchman a salaried servant of Government. Next came Mr. D. J. Macneile's Report in 1866, asking for the total abolition of the village watch and for placing villages under the jurisdiction of the regular police, whose numbers were to be increased for this purpose. None of these proposals met with favour, and the Act of 1870 had to be devised on more or less fresh lines.

14. The main principle of the Act may be represented as the "municipalization" of the village police, meaning its reconstitution as an organ of the village community, paid by, and responsible to, the community acting through a representative committee called the *panchayat*. In the words of "The Statement of Objects and Reasons of the Act" (*Calcutta Gazette*, 1870, p. 357), "the provisions of the Bill, while maintaining the responsibility of all landholders to report crime, are based upon principles which have been recognized as applicable to these Provinces, first, that it is just and expedient that the people at large should pay for their own protection; and secondly, that it is the duty and policy of the Government to leave as much as possible of the business of the country to be done by the people themselves." The members of the *panchayat* were nominated by the district magistrate, and before a committee was appointed in any village, it was his duty either personally or through a subordinate to explain to the villagers the object of the measure, and seek to enlist their co-operation. The *panchayat* were given power to fix the salaries of watchmen and the number to be employed in each village. They assessed and collected the necessary funds. They had also power to appoint and dismiss watchmen. The *panchayat* worked under the general control of the magistrate, but this control was not to be exercised unless there had been neglect or failure on the part of the *panchayat* to take the necessary action. Besides the general control of the magistrate, there were three means open to Govern-

ment for checking abuses: first, the power given to the magistrate to fine anyone who refused to act on the *panchayat*; secondly, the provision by which a *panchayat* who refused to collect the amount required for the watchmen's salary might have their goods and chattels distrained to make up the amount; thirdly, the power reserved to the Lieutenant-Governor to frame rules which would have the force of law for the guidance of *panchayats*. The idea behind these measures was evidently to bring back to life, as far as possible, the state of things supposed to have been in existence before the large landholders or the Government stepped in to assume the rights of the village community.

15. The Act had not long been in operation before complaints were heard. These complaints were summarized by the Bengal Police Committee (1891) as follows[1]: First, though there was some improvement in the wages of village watchmen since the Act, the improvement was due not to the *panchayats* but entirely to the action of magistrates. Secondly, there was everywhere the greatest reluctance among villagers to serve on *panchayats*, due (1) to the appointment being compulsory, of indefinite duration, unremunerative, and entailing great personal trouble and responsibility; (2) to *panchayats* being liable to great odium and enmity among their fellow-villagers if they collected dues punctually or distrained and sold for arrears; (3) to growing police interference with the affairs of *panchayats*, though this was not contemplated in the Act. Thirdly, owing to the unpopularity of the *panchayats* the best men were out of them, and their efficiency and reputation suffered in consequence. Fourthly, the assessments levied by *panchayats* were in many cases unfair, rich or influential people being let off with only a light contribution, while the poorer villagers were heavily assessed. These failures soon

[1] *Report*, paras. 16–20.

began to tell, and within fifteen years of the passing of the Act a fresh change was demanded—from the municipal idea to something of the idea of a regular state police. The remarks of the Police Commission (1902–3) on this change of opinion deserve notice: "A fair trial can hardly be said to have been given to the village system. The Commission have also formed the impression that, with some striking exceptions, there is too little interest in the village police displayed by collectors in this Province. . . . The Commission are disposed to attribute the failure of the *panchayat* system in some measure at least to this lack of interest."[1]

16. The two principal amendments by legislative action to the Act of 1870 took place in 1886[2] and 1892.[3] The direction in which the reforming process was set by these amending Acts was somewhat to discountenance the village municipal system. Mr. Cotton (now Sir Henry Cotton), who introduced the Act of 1892 in the Legislative Council described the step as one "in the direction of centralizing police administration, and of bringing the village watch much more than it now is under the immediate supervision of the District Magistrate."[4] The main changes sanctioned in 1886 were these: (1) the *panchayats* were relieved of the duty of collecting the tax required for the maintenance of village police. They continued to assess the tax, but the actual collection was to be carried out by a paid agency working under the magistrate; (2) the *panchayats* were to retain the right of nominating watchmen, but the appointment itself was to be made by the magistrate; (3) the power of punishing and dismissing watchmen was to be withdrawn from *panchayats* and transferred to magistrates or Superintendents of Police; (4) the village watchmen were hereafter to receive only money salaries in every case. Any lands

[1] *Report*, ch. iii.
[2] Act i. (B.C.) of 1886.
[3] Act i. (B.C.) of 1892.
[4] Speech, April 23, 1892.

assigned for watchmen, still outstanding, were to be settled with the zemindar, the produce to go to a fund called the Village Watchmen's Fund. The Act of 1892 went further in the same direction: (1) it transferred from the *panchayat* to the magistrate the power to determine the number of watchmen in each village and to fix their salary; (2) it empowered the magistrate, at his own discretion, and not merely at the suggestion of a *panchayat*, to appoint a Government officer to take charge of the collection of taxes; (3) fines and penalties were to be credited not to a village fund, but to a district fund for maintaining village watchmen. Parallel with this curtailment of the powers of *panchayats*, the Act of 1892 introduced the rather radical change of allowing *panchayats* to be elected by the people "in any manner most convenient." The change amounted to this—a committee designed with the object of securing better popular representation was to undertake responsibilities of a manifestly lesser character. It is difficult to say the change has proved a success.

17. To sum up, the history of the village police in Bengal comprises the following successive stages—First, they started as an organ of the village community, responsible to its representatives. Secondly, during the Mughal period they tended increasingly to become the revenue and personal servants of the zemindars, the farmers of revenue. Thirdly, in 1793, Lord Cornwallis placed them by regulation under Government police officers, but they continued practically under the control of the zemindars. Fourthly, in 1870 they were put back into the position of village servants responsible to representative village committees. Fifthly, in 1886 and 1892 they were, to a considerable extent, removed from the control of village committees and placed under the immediate direction of the magisterial officers of Government.

18. In describing the present state of the village police in the different provinces, it is convenient to go back for a moment to the brief description of the ancient village watch with which this chapter began. It will be seen from that description that the village community had principally three organs of police administration, namely, the headman, the watchman, and the general body of villagers. Around these three factors may also be gathered the leading features of the present system. To take first the headman, he is still the head of the police in his village in almost every province except Bengal, or the greater part of Bengal. On the whole, his position may be described as that of an intermediary between the village police and the village community on the one hand, and the District Administration on the other, any interference by the regular police in the internal affairs of the village being, as a rule, steadily discountenanced. It is to him that the watchmen make their reports, and reports to the regular constabulary are usually made by him. The Criminal Procedure Code lays on him, in the first instance, the duty of reporting to the magistrate or the police such matters as the whereabouts of notorious thieves, the commission of serious offences in the village, the occurrence of unnatural deaths, etc. It also empowers the District Magistrate, where there are no headmen, to appoint them specifically for the purpose of this section.[1] The first report of an offence committed in a village which the headman forwards to a magistrate is often of great importance in the judicial inquiry which arises over the offence. Variations between the headman's story and subsequent accounts are a usual form of assistance to defence counsel. Almost invariably the headman combines revenue with police duties. The justification of the system has been stated to be the increased knowledge

[1] Sec. 45.

of the village, which comes of doing revenue duties, the prestige and influence he thereby commands in the village, and the manifest economy of employing one officer for this double function. The arrangement is in accordance with the well-known views of Sir T. Munro. It is urged, on the other hand, that this makes him too much a tool of the Revenue Department, and that oftentimes his other duties take up so much of his attention as to leave him little time for police work. While his position is of greater consequence in Madras, Bombay, and Burma than in any other province, it may be said on the whole that there is a general resemblance in most provinces. On the general character of the village headman as an officer of police, the following words from a Resolution of the United Provinces Government in 1910 are instructive.[1] "The village headman is for the most part what the district officer makes him, and the success or failure of the system lies in the hands of those who administer it. At the best, the village headman can be a most useful connecting link between the police and the people, who can give assistance to the former and smooth the path of the latter. He can increase the efficiency and the honesty of police work in villages, can mitigate popular prejudice, and remove misunderstandings. But at the worst, he will be the jackal of the least scrupulous members of the force."

19. In Madras the position of the village police was formally settled by a Regulation of 1816,[2] passed on the recommendation of a Commission of which Sir Thomas Munro was a member. Its effect was to place the village watchmen under the control of the Revenue and Magisterial Officers, but to recognize the headman as the local authority. A subsequent Act passed in 1859, to organize the present regular police, left the village watch in the same position as before, and with

[1] *United Provinces Police Report*, 1910, Orders of Government.
[2] Reg. xi. of 1816.

a few secondary changes, the Regulation of 1816 has continued to this day. The police duties of the headman are set out in detail in the *Madras Village Officers' Manual*. Briefly, he "must maintain law and order in his village, applying for assistance to higher authorities if necessary, and reporting to them the occurrence of crimes and the movements of criminal gangs."[1] An important change in the responsibility of village headmen as police officers has taken place in Madras, as in some other provinces, within recent years by the abolition of what was known as the *Village Beat System*. This was an arrangement by which constables of the regular police used to be told off to watch village areas in addition to the old village police. Its abolition has practically left the headman as the undisputed head of the police within his jurisdiction. An increased sense of responsibility is hoped for in consequence, and to a certain extent has in fact been shown. An examination of the official reports points to three defects as regards the general character of headmen as police functionaries: (1) their illiteracy; (2) their tendency to be mixed up in local quarrels; and (3) their occasional alliance with criminal tribes—an analysis which will be found to apply to other provinces besides Madras.

20. In Bombay the village police were placed for the first time under the District Magistrate in 1852. The change was declared to have worked satisfactorily, and the Village Police Act of 1867, which still regulates the organization of the village police, confirmed the change and formulated the duties of the officers concerned. The head of the police in the village is an officer called the *police patel*, who very often combines the office with the duty of revenue collection. He is often, in fact, the village headman in another guise. His duties correspond in the main to the police duties of the headman in Madras. Besides the supervision of

[1] *Imperial Gazetteer of India*, vol. iv, p. 281.

the village police and the maintenance of order, he is "to furnish the magistrate of the district with any returns or information called for, and to keep him constantly informed as to the state of crime and all matters connected with the village police and the health and general condition of the community in his village."[1] Certain improvements were effected in his position on the recommendation of the Police Commission of 1902–3. They have been summarized as follows: (*a*) Greater subordination of the village servants to the *patel*; (*b*) instruction to magistrates that they should refer to the *patels* any people who come to them with complaints of petty hurt and abuse; (*c*) investing selected *patels* with special powers to try petty cases on the spot.[2] The position in Sind, which forms part of the Bombay Presidency, is that there is nothing there which may be properly called a village police, and the duties which elsewhere are performed by headmen are done by local landowners, "most of whom loyally give the assistance of their great influence to the police in all criminal cases." The attempt to create an official class of headmen has not materialized (1912) owing to the unwillingness of landowners to be enrolled as paid Government servants and to the possibility of discontent among them where one man is singled out in an area comprising numerous influential men.[3] The headmen in Burma, who are a creation of Government, have important police duties, which are set out in detail in the Burma Village Act.[4]

21. In the landlord villages of Upper India, the duties of the headman are discharged by one of the landlords specially selected. Taking first the United Provinces, the landlords shared among them for a long time the responsibilities of village police. These

[1] *Bombay Administration Report*, 1911–12, pp. 28–9.
[2] *Bombay Police Report*, 1910, pp. 20–1.
[3] *Bombay Administration Report*, 1911–12, p. 30.
[4] Act. vi. of 1907, secs. 7 and 8.

responsibilities, which had been enforced by regulation till 1862, were from that year enforced under the Criminal Procedure Code (sec. 45). This provision, as will be remembered, authorized District Magistrates to appoint headmen for the purpose of reporting crime, where the village itself did not provide for it. Rules were issued under this section in 1895 with the object of setting up the *lambardar*, who is merely a representative of the landlords for revenue dealings with Government, as headman for the purpose of the Criminal Procedure Code. If he was not a resident in the village, some other influential landlord was appointed. The headmen thus chosen, who are called *mukhiyas*, have no police duties apart from the Procedure Code, which amount practically to communicating information on specific topics, and to little more. In the Punjab the *lambardar* has the primary responsibility not merely for communicating information, but for maintaining the peace of the village. In some villages there are more than one of these representative landlords, in which case one of them is selected as chief (*ala-lambardar*). These men are under the control of an officer in charge of a group of villages, called a *zaildar* or *inamdar*. In the Central Provinces, of which the greater part consists of landlord villages, the *lambardar* is, as a rule, constituted headman (*mukaddam*) for the general administration of the village, and his duties are defined by the Land Revenue Act. He is responsible "for reporting crime and for assisting the police." In villages of small holders (*ryotwari*) the village *patel* is in charge of the police, and discharges in respect of it the same duties as the headman of a landlord village.

22. The position of the village watchman is less complex than that of the headman, and is more easily described. His functions extend "to the arrest of offenders, general aid to the police, the maintenance of a watch over bad characters and suspicious persons, and

the general supply of local information."[1] Sir Murray Hammick, when he was Inspector-General of Police in Madras, summarized the duties of the watchman as follows: (1) Patrol of the village; (2) surveillance of strangers; (3) execution of criminal processes; and (4) the carrying of information to police stations.[2] The methods of remunerating village watchmen fall into two classes applicable, in widely varying proportions, to most provinces—either by assignments of land and grain-fees, or by monthly salaries in cash. In Bombay and the Central Provinces the old custom of land assignment and grain-fees prevails almost exclusively. The money required in the case of the salary system is largely raised by means of a local cess, to which sometimes non-agriculturists also have to contribute. The Police Commission of 1902–3 seemed on the whole to favour the first form of remuneration. In their opinion the advantages of the system are these: In the case of an assignment of land, the watchman is provided with occupation for his spare time and for his family, and reaps what may be called the moral benefits of an agricultural life. Grain-fees keep the watchman in communication with the agriculturists, and give him a sense of obligation to them. In making the appointments, hereditary claims are always respected, but the appointments themselves are, as a rule, made by the magistrate on the nomination of headmen and landowners. In some parts of the country there are no rural policemen who may be properly so called. In the Central Provinces, for example, the watchmen are in the position almost entirely of the headman's personal servants, and all of them may be summoned by him for police duties, and any one of them may be called in to help in any village duty. In Burma the only kind of functionaries who may be called rural policemen are what are called the "ten-

[1] *Imperial Gazetteer of India*, vol. iv, ch. 12, p. 39.
[2] *Statement of Police Committee on District Police in Madras*, 1902, sec. 2, para. 153.

house men" in Lower Burma[1] and the agents of outlying hamlets in Upper Burma.[2] In Assam there are rural policemen appointed on the Bengal model in the Surma Valley and in Goalpara. In Sind what corresponds to a village police is the class of trackers known as *pagis*, who are skillful in tracing stolen animals by their footprints. They were a necessary appendage in an unsettled time to an agricultural community with a scattered population. Sir Bartle Frere, in a memorandum on the Sind police in 1859, said of them: "I have known some of the more experienced ones make a very good livelihood, equal to ten or twelve rupees per mensem. It is esteemed an honourable profession, and in disputes the word of an experienced tracker is often regarded as decisive; I have known robbers appeal to it, and admit their guilt at once and show where the stolen property was concealed, if the tracker's fiat were against them."[3] Originally their employment was casual, but now some of them receive regular employment in *talukas* and villages at the rate of Rs. 10 and Rs. 5 per mensem.[4]

23. The policy with regard to village watchmen is as strongly as ever against placing them in direct subordination to the regular police. Their responsibility is to the magistrate and the Revenue Department through the village local authorities. Whilst this arrangement has certainly its own faults, it must be recognized that it is preferable to the other system of making them a part of the regular constabulary. The Revenue Officials, though subject necessarily to the routine of the Department, are yet interested in the preservation of the village as the administrative unit, and there is less danger under them than under the Police Department of the functionaries of the village being absorbed into a centralized administration. At

[1] *Se-ein-gaungs.* [2] *Ywa-gaungs.*
[3] *Memorandum on the Sind Police*, H. B. E. Frere, 1859.
[4] *Bombay Administration Report*, 1911–12, p. 30.

the same time it is recognized to be a prime necessity that though not subordinate to the regular police, they must give them every possible co-operation, and it is an object of care on the part of those responsible that this relation of co-operation between the two arms of the police is sustained and promoted. One of the strongest advocates of the present system was Sir Murray Hammick as Inspector-General of Police in Madras, and to his influence is largely due the strong stand which that Government have since taken in the preservation of village institutions. It is interesting, however, to note two little changes in recent years which appear, somewhat unconsciously, to go against this idea. The first is the providing of village watchmen in increasing numbers with official badges and staves to signify their authority. This is to give them an appearance of aloofness from the village, and to present them as less of a natural organ of the village community. Another change is an occasional instance of what are known as *talayaris*' meetings, which means the gathering of watchmen in a particular group of villages to meet the Government Sub-Inspector of Police and receive instructions from him. Fortunately the practice is being discountenanced.[1]

24. Coming to the action of the village community as a whole, the first thing to note is that the ancient joint responsibility of villages for crime occurring in their areas is still enforced, though rarely, in provinces such as Burma, the Punjab and Sind by the levy of a fine on the whole village, which is collected usually as if it were a revenue demand. It is customary also on occasions to offer a reward to a whole village in the form of a money present or of a remission of revenue if good work has been done in preventing or discovering crime.[2] There is provision in many provinces requiring the inhabitants of villages to give assistance to villagers

[1] *Madras Police Report*, 1912–13, Orders of Government.

[2] *Punjab Police Report*, 1906, Orders of Government, para. 7.

in resisting robberies or similar aggression. Another way in which the community takes part in police work is by the institution of *panchayats* for furnishing information to the regular police regarding the existence of bad characters in the village.[1] There is, on the other hand, in parts of the Punjab a strong organized combination in villages *against* giving evidence to the police. The combination is cemented by each member taking an oath to uphold it at whatever cost, called "*Dua Khair*."[2] Apart from these more or less normal modes of proceeding, the village communities make special organized efforts, when a grave necessity arises, for joint police action. A few of the more conspicuous instances of such common action may be noticed.

25. One of the most noteworthy of such instances is what is known as the *Tikri Chaukidari* system in the Amritsar district in the Punjab. It was employed with satisfactory results in 1897, during a period of exceptional outbursts of robbery. The Punjab Police Report for 1898[3] contains a good account of the system, which may be quoted in full. "It is an arrangement under which all the villagers voluntarily undertake, in turn, to guard the entrances of the village at night. The method of selection for the duty is that two *gharras*, or large earthen vessels, ordinarily used for carrying water, are sunk in the ground in the place of the village common resort, the *patwar-Khano*, or the *dharmsala*, the neck and mouths of the *gharras* are left above ground-level, and are fastened with a lid secured by a lock. The names of all the male inhabitants of the village, irrespective of caste or position, and who are between certain stated ages, are written on scraps of paper—whence the name *tikri*; these are folded, and all the names are then dropped into one of the receptacles, the whole are well stirred up. A number of stout cudgels, called *lathis* or *dangs*, are provided, which cor-

[1] *Madras Police Report*, 1912–13, para. 8.
[2] *Punjab Police Report*, 1907, para. 7.
[3] Para. 28.

respond in number with the number of watchmen that the village community has decided shall be nightly on duty : these cudgels are the batons of office. Daily the village elders and such persons interested as care to attend meet at the place where the name receptacles are, the lock is opened, papers to the number of watchmen for duty on the approaching night are drawn at hazard, and the cudgels of office are then despatched to the persons whose names have been drawn, and it becomes the duty of each one to undertake in person watch on the night. The names after having been drawn are dropped into the second receptable, and those who have done a night's watch are no more liable until all have had their turn, when the business commences over again." The system has more recently declined almost into abeyance, partly because the necessity for it has become less pressing. There have been proposals to revive it by placing it on a legal basis. If the proposals were carried out, it would be interesting to know whether the improvement expected has really been brought about by compulsion. The question looks rather like *Conscription against Voluntaryism* ; and in the absence of reliable information as to what the village Tories and Radicals of Amritsar, in moments of fierce party war, are apt to say on this question in the blazing purlieus of the village parliament, we must be content to quote the following from the sober report of an officer of the Civil Service.[1] "The effect of the *Tikri Chaukidari* system in Amritsar seems to be waning. It is natural that when people discover that there is no legal punishment for neglect, they should become negligent. I see no reason why we should not enforce village responsibility for the prevention of crime by legalizing the system. The crux of the whole matter is probably the decision of who are and who are not liable to be put on the

[1] Sir J. M. Douie, *Punjab Police Report*, 1898, para 28.

roster. The work of watch and ward is the proper task of the young unmarried men. Having regard to the conditions of village life, I do not think we can expect much service of this sort from married men, at least of the landowning classes." [1]

26. Two other cases may be noted. A system adopted for organized resistance of robbers in a Central Provinces district in 1883, at the instance of a magistrate, was thus described by him. "I had lists prepared of all able-bodied men in every village, and ordered that, on the approach of dacoits, an alarm should be sounded, whereupon all whose names appeared in these lists were to collect at some previously arranged place with all available arms, and to combine in the defence of the village, instead of flying in every direction, as they usually did. . . . In addition to this, red paper discs were issued to the *Mukaddam* (headman) of every village, with instructions that on the receipt of information as to the movements of the dacoits, that information should be at once forwarded, written on the backs of these discs, to all the surrounding villages, who were to pass the information on promptly, at the same time turning out *en masse* over the whole of their respective village areas, to watch for any further movements on the part of the dacoits. This method of spreading information is one well known and understood in the country." [2] A somewhat similar system was employed in Bombay in 1899, during a time of prolonged agricultural scarcity. The village police and *patels*, with as many able-bodied, willing villagers as they could get were encouraged to pass the nights, particularly during the dark half of the month, in the village *chavadis* (meeting-house) with a supply of slings, stones, and sticks handy, the men more or less on the alert,

[1] A certain resemblance may perhaps be traced between the *Tikri Chaukidari* system and the liability of citizens to serve as special constables in England in a time of emergency.

[2] *Central Provinces Police Report*, 1883, para. 64.

at any rate prepared to give the dacoits a warm reception. The Inspector-General of Police said in his report: "The effect on the crime returns from action of this sort has been extremely encouraging. In most villages I have found the people are quite alive to the advantages to be looked for from concerted action of the kind, and a sufficient number are generally found ready and willing to take their turn."[1]

27. In this connection reference may be made also to the levy system in Baluchistan, started by Sir Robert Sandeman for the security of the country and the frontier. It consisted of a small number of tribal horsemen taken into Government service, but was subsequently extended by "offering the headmen allowances for maintaining a certain number of armed horse and foot, by whose means they were expected to keep order in their tribes and to produce offenders when crime occurred."[2]

[1] *Bombay Police Report*, 1900, para. 12.
[2] *Imperial Gazetteer of India*, vol. iv, p. 334.

CHAPTER VII

ADMINISTRATION OF JUSTICE

1. THE usual method of settling differences in the old village community was by referring them for arbitration to the headman, who settled small disputes himself but secured the assistance of a council of elders in determining more important matters. The headman possessed also powers of criminal justice, which though often enough in the disorganization of later times he exercised with some degree of oppression, he was restrained and moderated by the influence of village opinion. The duty which the headman and the *panchayat* felt in any case submitted to them seems primarily to have been rather to find a means for composing differences and satisfying both parties than to award a decree in favour of one and to leave the other an absolute loser. Nearly all the reports of early British Administrators in India speak of the headman as the main judicial authority of the village. The *Fifth Report* (1812) mentions among his various duties in Madras the "settling of the disputes of the inhabitants."[1] Elphinstone recognized him, in 1821, in the territories under the rule of the Peshwa as the primary authority for settling disputes in the village.[2] The Court of *Sadr Dewani Adalat*[3] in Bengal, in a report on the judicial powers of headmen, said (1827): "We are decidedly of opinion that every encourage-

[1] Pp. 84, 85. [2] *Report on the Territories Conquered from the Paishwa*, p. 26.
[3] Principal civil court.

ment should be given to . . . the heads of villages to arbitrate and settle *as heretofore* any trivial disputes between the inhabitants of their respective villages, which may be voluntarily submitted to their adjustment and award."[1]

2. The procedure adopted by the headman must have been exceedingly irregular and informal; and even if a fairly definite system could be traced in any particular area, it must have varied considerably from the system which obtained in other parts. The only reports available which deal in any detail with the question are confined to Western India, to the regions which passed under Maratha rule. Elphinstone thus described the procedure in a suit for the recovery of a debt. "If a complaint was made to a *patel*, he would send for the person complained of, and if he admitted the debt, would interfere partly as a friend to settle the mode and time of payment. If the debt were disputed, and he and his *kulkarni* could not by their own influence or sagacity effect a settlement to the satisfaction of both parties, the *patel* assembled a *panchayat* of inhabitants of the village, who inquired into the matter with very little form, and decided as they thought best; but this decision could not take place without the previous consent of the parties. If the complainant were refused a *panchayat* or disapproved of the decision, or if he thought proper not to apply to the *patel*, he went to the *Mamlatdar* who proceeded nearly in the same manner as the *patel*, with this addition—that he could compel the party complained of to submit it to a *panchayat*, or else make satisfaction to a complainant."[2] The method of administering criminal justice was stated in Mr. Chaplin's Report on the Deccan (1824) as follows: "*Patels* exercised formerly without any defined limits to their authority the power of slightly punishing for all minor offences, such as abusive

[1] *Report of Select Committee*, 1832, App. H.
[2] *Report on the Territories Conquered from the Paishwa*, p. 76.

language, petty assaults, and trespasses. The punishment seldom went beyond a few blows with the open hand or confinement for a couple of days in the village *choultry*, the prisoner paying subsistence money to the *havildar*, or peon, who was placed over him. A *Musala*, or fine, was perhaps occasionally exacted, which did not, however, exceed a rupee and a quarter; the rupee going to the *sirkar* and the rest to the *havildar*. If the crime were of such a nature as to require the infliction of a greater penalty, the delinquent was sent to the *mamlatdar* for trial."[1] To the same effect was a report by the Collector of Ahmednagar (1827): "The heads of villages still have and do exercise the power of confining persons who are guilty of crimes till they can report about them, of chastising petty delinquents to the extent of a few stripes, and of forcing the ryots to pay their rents by the usual means of *tukhuza*, such as setting the defaulter in the sun, putting a stone on his head, etc."[2]

3. The authority of *panchayats* was, as a rule, confined to important civil cases. They were probably not fixed local tribunals, but were appointed for the adjudication of each particular dispute for which their services were required. The duty of constituting and summoning a *panchayat* probably lay with the headman, but in a village he was often bound, if not to accept, at least to consider, the wishes of the parties. No one, however, felt bound to submit a dispute to a *panchayat*, but whenever it was decided to submit one, it was customary to enter into an agreement to abide by the award. The agreement was sometimes put in writing, but was often sealed by the making of a sign. There was no definite limit to the number of members; it might range from five or less to fifty or more. The usual place of meeting was under a tree or in the village temple or *choultry*. There was no direct

[1] *Report on the Deccan*, W. Chaplin, 1824, p. 142.
[2] *Report of Select Committee*, 1832, App. M.

remuneration offered for the services of the members. The chief motives which led men to accept the position were the obvious respectability attaching to it, the chance of a present from one or both of the parties, and the desire to avoid the odium of shirking a public duty. The proceedings were thoroughly informal, and took the form of an animated conversation in which more people than one took part at the same time. If in any case it was thought necessary to commit the award to writing, it was left to be done by the village accountant.[1] The intimate local knowledge of the judges was generally sufficient to secure a tolerable degree of justice in the awards; and the strength of communal opinion in the village often guaranteed the performance of the verdict. On the whole, the village communities were not subjected to interference, and their verdicts were final, though interference was not altogether unknown in notorious cases. On the apparent resemblance between a *panchayat* and a jury, Holt Mackenzie made this statement before the Select Committee of 1831–2: "The *panchayat* can scarcely in its native shape be said to bear any distinct analogy to a jury, being, in fact, merely a body of men to whom a cause is generally referred. They are not bound to decide; there is no issue given to them to try; they are under no direction, and are left to scramble out of their case as best they can."

4. The chief advantage of a *panchayat* was, of course, the obligation which the very nature of the tribunal threw upon parties and witnesses to tell the truth. In a small concentrated community, it was not likely that any one who cared to live a comfortable life would venture an untruth before a council of his fellows. Sleeman, in his *Rambles and Recollections*,[2] has an interesting comment on the difficulty he sometimes

[1] Elphinstone, p. 78.

[2] *Rambles and Recollections of an Indian Official*, Sleeman, Constable, 1893, vol. ii, ch. ii, pp. 34–5.

felt in arriving at the truth in cases in which *sepoys* were involved, "and yet, I believe, there are no people in the world from whom it is more easy to get it in their own village communities where they state it before their relations, elders and neighbours, whose esteem is necessary to happiness and can be obtained only by an adherence to truth." Another advantage which must have helped the long continuance of the system was that in the greater or lesser degree of isolation in which village communities often found themselves, there was no other tribunal of any competence before which disputes could be easily lodged. Moreover, the local authority and knowledge of the elders rendered the *panchayat* in ordinary cases—that is, in cases which did not entail undue labour—"clear and prompt in its decision."[1] And this was helped by the additional circumstance that so long as a *panchayat* held its sitting, its members were being kept from the more insistent work of earning their daily bread and so were not likely to brook "needless complaint or affected delay."[2] But it is noted that they were apt to be dilatory in cases where the matter before them involved the examination of some laborious and intricate account. Then "it adjourns frequently; when it meets again, some of the members are often absent, and it sometimes happens that a substitute takes the place of an absent member."[3] The chief weakness of the *panchayat* was probably the absence of sufficient power to carry through the necessary preliminaries to a judicial proceeding, such as seizing the defendant and summoning witnesses. Perhaps also, when the members of a *panchayat* were appointed, as often happened, by the parties themselves, the fact that they would try to play the part rather of advocates than of judges might have caused difficulty.

[1] Minute on the state of the Country, etc., Munro, December 31, 1824.
[2] Elphinstone, p. 88.
[3] Minute on the state of the Country, etc., Munro, December 31, 1824.

5. For some time during the early years of British rule, there appears to have been a definite attempt made, with a degree of enthusiasm which differed with each locality and the individual officers concerned, to make use in an informal way of the old *panchayat* system. It is clear that from the beginning there was a somewhat strong feeling among the officers of the East India Company against the institution of *panchayats* in ordinary disputes, but their usefulness in the determination of purely social questions such as those relating to caste and of revenue matters, was recognized. The question was gone into at some length by the Select Committee on East India affairs in 1831–2, and their evidence bears out the foregoing statement. A civil servant from Madras[1] gave the following account: "I have had considerable experience of the use of *panchayats* as a revenue officer in the Bellary Division of the Ceded Districts, and found them exceedingly useful there in adjusting matters of dispute, both between the inhabitants themselves and between myself as the representative of the Government and the ryots paying land revenue, as well as the merchants; I have often found the parties resist all argument on the part of my native servants as well as of myself, but immediately concede the point with cheerfulness when decided in favour of the Government by a *panchayat*. . . . In such cases, as well as in numerous disputes regarding village offices, such as the right to the privileges of the head of the village or of the watchman or other village officers, *panchayats* have been most extensively employed by the revenue officers in Bellary. . . . In the *Ryotwari* settled districts, such as Bellary, there are constantly in attendance at the offices of the Collectors and Magistrates many hundreds, sometimes thousands, of the ryots, particularly at the period of the annual settlements, when occasionally 10,000 to 12,000

[1] A. D. Campbell.

people of that description may be congregated together at the same time. The parties themselves are left to select out of those bodies of people whom they choose, and the Collector generally nominates one of the leading agricultural inhabitants, known to be a person of good sense and discrimination, care being invariably taken to ascertain from both parties that he is one to whom neither have any objection. If a case were between a lender of money and a borrower of it, the *panchayat* would consist in all probability of two wealthy monied men, chosen by the native banker, two respectable cultivators chosen by the ryot, and a fifth person of the description above mentioned, selected by the Collector. A great deal in a *panchayat* depends upon the proper selection of the fifth person; the other persons enter into violent disputes and the fifth acts as the moderator. Some of the decrees drawn up by *panchayats* at Bellary are admirable specimens of native intelligence, seldom equalled by some of our own European decrees. The members are never paid. They are not sworn. Even intricate disputes in the revenue department are settled at least in the course of a single day. Where the parties agree to settle a dispute by *panchayat*, there is no limitation in amount—the decision is final except on the proof of partiality or corruption of members."

6. In the Bombay Presidency, Elphinstone had laid down in 1821: "Our principal instrument must continue to be the *panchayat*, and that must continue to be exempt from all new forms, interference, and regulation on our part."[1] In the rules for the regulation of *panchayats* in the Southern Maratha Country (as given in the Appendix to a Minute by Sir John Malcolm in 1829),[2] all causes relating to the internal regulations of particular castes were to be exclusively settled by *panchayats* composed of members of the caste concerned.

[1] *Report*, p. 99.
[2] Minute on the Revenue and Judicial Administration of the Southern Mahratta Country, April 23, 1829.

All causes relating to the following subjects were to be referred to *panchayats* for adjustment, unless the parties agreed to bring their suit before a *Munsif*: (1) religion, (2) marriage, (3) peculiar customs of places, (4) *Wuttuns* or *Huks*,[1] (5) division of property, (6) maintenance, (7) old and intricate accounts, (8) disputes between two inhabitants of the same village within the sum of 50 rupees, personal property or value, (9) suits for damages for alleged personal injuries and for personal damages of whatever nature, (10) boundary disputes. These *panchayats* worked under the general superintendence of the *Amildar*. He forwarded the decrees to the Collector, by whom they were referred to the chief law officer, Hindu or Muhammadan, of the religion of the parties concerned. If he approved, the Collector set his seal and signature to the decree and carried it into execution. Appeals were allowed, though rarely, to a superior *panchayat* (*Sir-Punnah*) if sufficient primary grounds were shown. The establishment of regular courts and forms of justice was leading to a great decline in the influence of *panchayats*, "but these are still universally resorted to in cases of arbitration and in the small causes that come under the jurisdiction of the village officers. They are also resorted to to fix the settlement of disputes about caste or religion, and are . . . generally well employed in fixing the details of the amount of revenue assessment."

7. The following extract from Holt Mackenzie's evidence before the Select Committee (1831–2) describes the use made of *panchayats* in Upper India. It will be noticed that with the system of joint land-holding communities which prevailed there, their use in revenue matters was more often to settle rights as between different village communities than among members of the same community. "In cases relating to questions of caste, they are frequently very

[1] Hereditary estates or rights.

numerous. Revenue officers have used the *panchayat.* I believe the native collectors use it extensively to adjust various disputes between the village communities and the different members of such communities. The collectors too frequently have recourse to it in the determination of questions of private right when making settlements. One officer in particular, with whom I had made much communication and who is singularly well acquainted with the natives of the country where he has been (Mr. W. Fraser) systematically employed it to a great extent in settling the boundary disputes between villages, preparatory to the survey of the Delhi territory and the districts immediately adjoining, and he stated that he had found the plan very successful, having obtained the decision of 300 cases in that way. . . . His scheme was partly on the principle of a jury, and partly on that of the *panchayat*, that is, the members were generally chosen on the nomination of the parties, but they were required to decide without delay; the matter in dispute was brought to a distinct issue, and the whole proceedings were regularly recorded by a Government clerk who was deputed for the purpose. The disputes were generally between (what I may call republican) communities of yeomen cultivating their own fields, for the possession of land generally of little value, but very eagerly contested by the people. The headmen of the contending villages, acting for, and in the presence of, the whole body, were required to nominate six on each side, making on the whole twelve. The right of challenge was freely allowed, and the jury (so to term it) was required to be unanimous. Mr. Fraser's reason for having so many as twelve was, as he said, chiefly that they might, by their number and weight, be placed above the reach of intimidation or danger from the vengeance of those against whom they might decide; and it was with the same view also, with that of putting down party spirit, that he required unanimity."

8. A highly unfavourable account of the way in which *panchayats* were worked in Bundlekand under former governments was given by an official of the Company who served there, and was reproduced in a letter from the Bengal Government to the Court of Directors (1827).[1] It is extremely difficult at this stage to pronounce an opinion on the general truth of this report, but it is at least interesting as a spicy account of what to a British official at the time seemed the possible misdoings of an ill-controlled *panchayat.* "Under the former government of this district, the superintendence or management of *panchayats* was never from the earliest times that I have been able to trace confined to any particular individuals or body of men whatever, and the consequence was that they were very often either futile in their results or terminated in a murderous conflict between the parties and their adherents. The selection of the arbitrators proceeded always from the disputants themselves, and they were chosen generally from the most respectable of the tribe or profession to which the parties belonged. If the subject was rent, the head *zemindars* or *canongoes* were generally chosen, but residents of neighbouring villages were commonly referred to their own townsmen. Boundary disputes were settled in the same way, and a large assemblage of men from all the surrounding villages were often invited by the parties to witness the settlement. This almost invariably led to violent affrays and the loss of many lives, and which again branched out into innumerable feuds, laying the foundations of continued disorder and bloodshed. The officers of the former Government seldom interfered, until matters got to such extremes as to endanger the realization of their revenue, which was the primary, I may say, the only object of their care; they then interposed their influence to bring about a final adjust-

[1] *Report of Select Committee*, 1832, App. H.

ment of the dispute. . . . As the disputes connected with land and its produce were generally settled by *panchayats* composed of *zemindars* or *canongoes* . . . so were the claims and accounts of bankers settled by arbitrators, consisting of the most respectable of that profession, and the same obtained with other professions; but the habits of those classes being more peaceable than those of the *zemindars*, the greatest evil arising from the inefficiency of the system with respect to them, lay in the frequent futility of the award, from inability to enforce it."

9. Besides the employment of informal village *panchayats*, there are a few provinces which have tried the experiment of incorporating the institution by law in the regular judicial system. One of the earliest to start it was Madras, where, under the influence of Sir Thomas Munro, a regulation was passed in 1816[1] permitting the trial of cases by *panchayats.* This regulation still remains on the statute-book, however little it has been put to any real use. It was passed, in the words of the preamble, "with a view to diminish the expense of litigation and to render the principal and more intelligent inhabitants useful and respectable, by employing them in administering justice to their neighbours." The right of summoning a *panchayat* is left to the village headman; but this right is to be exercised only in cases where both the parties to a suit agree to submit the dispute to a *panchayat*, and where they do, there is to be no limitation in the amount or value of the suit. The *panchayat* must consist always of an odd number, never less than five nor more than eleven, and the majority shall decide. It must be composed of the most respectable inhabitants of the village, who shall be called upon to serve in rotation whenever their number is sufficient for the purpose. Any inhabitant who refuses may be fined. Where the

[1] Reg. v. of 1816.

parties belong to different castes the headman must nominate an equal number of each caste and complete the *panchayat* by the selection of a person or persons who belong to neither caste. There is to be no appeal from the award of a village *panchayat*. But in cases of gross partiality, the matter may be taken by petition to the District Judge. If the latter is convinced of partiality, he must refer the whole matter to the Court of Appeal, who may annul the decision and refer it to another *panchayat*; and where this second *panchayat* agrees with the first, the matter is settled finally. The depositions of witnesses are to be taken down in writing, on paper or on *cadjan* leaves,[1] in cases of above the value of 20 rupees. The parties are exempt from duties and fees of any kind, except the cost of the paper or leaves on which proceedings are written down.

10. Judged by its actual working, this regulation has proved almost a complete failure. Taking the period 1817–27, that is, the first eleven years following the passing of the regulation, village *panchayats* disposed of 738 cases in the first five years in the whole of the Presidency (or an average of 150 a year), and 199 in the last six years (or an average of 35).[2] Since then there has been no improvement whatever. In 1848[3] we get these figures :—

Cases disposed of	...	19
„ pending	...	16
		35

The Report on Civil Justice in 1880[4] mentions ten

[1] Palm leaves.

[2] *Report of Select Committee*, 1832, App. (2), Jud. iv.

[3] *Report, Civil Justice, Madras*, 1849, p. 6.

[4] Para. 101. *The Report on Civil Justice in Madras for* 1883, mentions a case valued at Rs. 5,307, which was decided by a village *panchayat* in the North Arcot District (para. 132); and the Report for 1884 mentions two cases before village *panchayats* in Salem, valued at Rs. 661 and Rs. 3,750 respectively (para. 127). But they were clearly exceptional.

cases as decided by village *panchayats*. The view of judicial authorities in Madras on this unpopularity of *panchayats* was thus put in 1829, in a report of the Court of *Sadr Adalat*: "Considering that parties in suits referred to village *panchayats* are not chargeable with any costs whatever, it was natural to expect that, with these advantages, arbitration would be more generally resorted to. The result of the experiment seems to warrant the conclusion that with the great mass of the people . . . its prevalence in former times was a matter of necessity, from the want of other tribunals, rather than the effect of a prepossession in favour of an ancient institution." The existence of other courts with rather slow and elaborate modes of procedure, composed of judges who did not know local matters too closely, was undoubtedly an incentive to a party conscious of a weak case to shun *panchayats*. But the constitution given to *panchayats* under the regulation was itself a cause. The old *panchayat* was a thoroughly informal affair. It took its own time, met where and when it liked, was ignorant of the blessedness of odd numbers and of decision by a majority, and was not as a rule accustomed to having its decrees annulled by a petition sent over the heads of its members. It must also be remembered that the headman was becoming increasingly rather a representative of the government than a man of the people; and the large powers given to him in the constitution and conduct of *panchayats* were not likely to impress the villagers with the popular character of the institution.

11. Within more recent years, in Madras, there have been instituted what are called Village Bench Courts under an Act of 1889.[1] This Act lays down primarily the civil judicial powers of the headman, who is empowered to try certain classes of suits, provided their value does not exceed twenty rupees, or if the

[1] *Madras Village Courts*, Act i. of 1889.

parties give their written consent to it, two hundred rupees. The headman's powers will be dealt with hereafter. The point to be noted here is that in every such case which the headman is empowered to try, it is open to either party to the suit to claim that it shall be tried by a Village Bench of three judges. One of these three judges is always the headman himself who acts as president, the other two are nominated by the parties out of a list prepared by the collector, of qualified residents in the village.[1] The essential distinction, if such a distinction can be made out, between a *panchayat* and a Bench Court would appear to be this, that the former looks upon arbitration as its primary duty, while the latter is rather concerned about adjudication in some form, not necessarily arbitration. The system has now been introduced into nearly every part of the province. The following figures will show the progress made :—

Year.		Cases.
[2] 1900	...	1167
[3] 1907	...	4117
[4] 1912	...	9935

These figures would indicate, so far as may be judged, a good amount of well sustained progress. But the remarks of district officers and of Government on it are, as a rule, cast in a tone of pessimism. An experienced officer of the Madras Civil Service,[5] in giving evidence before the Royal Commission on Decentralization, characterized as "disappointing" the working of Bench Courts. The reasons that he gave for this failure were three : (1) that there was a lack of interest on the part of superior officers of Government ; (2) that the ordinary jurisdiction of Bench Courts is the same as that of headman sitting singly, and so low

[1] Sec. 9.

[2] *Report, Civil Justice, Madras*, 1900, para. 20.

[3] *Ibid.*, 1907, para. 20.

[4] *Ibid.*, 1912, para. 7.

[5] H. W. Gillman, I.C.S.

that the members do not care to attend; (3) that the raising of the jurisdiction is only possible where parties mutually consent, but whenever they are prepared to consent, they also settle the matter themselves and do not trouble about going to court. The Government of Madras in their latest report apparently agree in thinking the Bench Courts unsuccessful.[1] The Madras High Court observed in 1912: "The extension of the Bench system offers the people of the village the best method of settling their disputes promptly and cheaply, and the Honourable Judges consider that every effort should be made to induce petty litigants to resort to these tribunals. The chief obstacles to success in this direction are the existence of faction in the village on the one hand, and the presence of law touts on the other. It is however hoped that primarily in the interests of the people themselves, and secondly as a relief to the congestion of the regular courts, the number of suits filed in these courts may continue to increase."[2]

12. In the Bombay Presidency the first attempt to use *panchayats* in the regular administration of justice was made by a Regulation of 1802, which was modified by a Regulation of 1827. As in Madras, the system almost entirely failed in actual working, and it was definitely abolished in 1861. Since then it has not been revived in the Bombay Presidency. A proposal to revive it was made by Mr. (now Sir William) Wedderburn, who was then District Judge of Ahmednagar, in connection with the serious agricultural disturbance which took place in the Deccan in 1875. The measure which was ultimately fixed upon is what is embodied in the Deccan Agriculturists' Relief Act (1879) for organizing, in selected areas, village courts presided over by village headmen. Sir William Wedderburn's proposal aimed, broadly, at appointing

[1] *Report, Civil Justice, Madras*, 1914, Orders of Government.
[2] *Ibid.*, 1912, para. 7.

arbitration boards or *panchayats* in place of courts presided over by headmen sitting singly. It had the support of a large body of educated Indian opinion in Bombay at the time, but although it received serious consideration in the Governor-General's Legislative Council, it was ultimately thrown out, chiefly on account of the strong opposition of the provincial Government in Bombay. The Government member in Calcutta, who was in charge of the Bill,[1] made the following statement on the proposal: "I must say frankly that I look upon as wholly visionary the idea that it is possible nowadays to find in every village or even in every small circle of villages, a body of men sufficient in number to allow selection from them by litigants for the formation of a *panchayat*, and at the same time qualified to be arbitrators by influence, intelligence, and absence of interest. And even were this otherwise, I should expect that the strict regulations, involving checks and delays, which the proposal just referred to comprises, would practically destroy the freedom, simplicity, and promptitude supposed to be the chief recommendations of the *panchayat* system."

13. More recently in the Punjab, a law has been passed (1912)[2] for the trial of civil cases by village *panchayats*. The Act has not been sufficiently long in operation for any reliable estimate of its results. Its main features are these. The appointment and summoning of *panchayats* are in the hands of the *district munsif* (the lowest civil judicial officer of Government). The consent of the parties must first be secured. The judgment of the *panchayat* is to be put on record. There is to be a small Court fee. The District Judge has the right to vary or set aside the decree of a *panchayat* if he thinks that a serious miscarriage of justice has resulted. The Local Government lays down rules regarding the qualifications and appoint-

[1] The Hon. T. C. Hope, Speech in the Imperial Legislative Council, October 24, 1879.

[2] VI. of 1912.

ment of members of *panchayats.* No legal practitioner is to be allowed to appear. *Panchayats* have no exclusive jurisdiction.

14. The idea of entrusting *criminal* cases to village *panchayats* was, perhaps alone among the provinces, put forward by the Punjab Government in 1912, about the same time as their other measure. There has been some doubt expressed by competent observers as to whether village *panchayats*, as a rule, had jurisdiction in criminal cases, and therefore if this measure passes into law, it will constitute an interesting step. For the present the Bill has been held in "suspended animation" till it is known how the *Civil Panchayats Act* works in practice. Sir Louis Dane, who as Lieutenant-Governor of the Punjab was responsible for the proposal, made a very suggestive speech on it in the Punjab Legislative Council, in which he traced the inspiration of the scheme chiefly to the example of Ireland, and in some measure also to that of Egypt. "For nearly two years I was a magistrate in a very remote agricultural district in the South-West of Ireland. It was my duty to sit with a great number of magistrates drawn from all classes of the community. . . . The magistrates are not all landed magnates—they are of all classes—shopkeepers, petty farmers, and exactly the sort of people who we contemplate in this country would sit upon these *panchayats.* . . . What often happens in such cases before a *panchayat* of magistrates—if I may call it a *panchayat*—in the South-West of Ireland is that a case which might have led to very high feeling and possibly given rise to a vendetta, even have led to murder, is disposed of by the magistrates sitting more or less as a body of conciliators . . . and by the process of conciliation the fount and origin of the quarrel are wiped out. . . . That is why I attach considerable importance to the action of the *panchayats* as conciliators if ever we can get them to work. Shortly after this measure came

before the Council . . . H.H. the Khedive introduced in Egypt what are known as Cantonal Courts. Now these Cantonal Courts . . . are exactly the same, to all intents and purposes, as the *panchayats* contemplated by us. Great stress is laid in Egypt upon the action of the Cantonal Courts as conciliators, and I understand from the papers and also from friends in Egypt . . . that although these Courts have only been in operation for six months, they show signs of giving the greatest satisfaction to the people in the disposal of agricultural disputes."[1] It may be pointed out that the Judges of the Punjab Chief Court were strongly opposed to criminal *panchayats*, chiefly for fear that increased facilities for administering criminal justice might spell an increase in petty accusations. Another reason was this: "The Judges view with great alarm the idea of entrusting wholly untrained, inexperienced, and often uneducated persons with no knowledge of law or of elementary principles of the administration of justice, with powers which, though in themselves apparently small, can be used to cause an infinite amount of injury."[2] It must be said that this sounds rather academic. In trying to compose differences in a petty criminal case between the complainant and the offender—in such a case, for example, as that A stole B's spade when B was away at the next village to find a husband for his daughter—it is conceivable that a village *panchayat* might get on without a knowledge of Analytical Jurisprudence.

15. Besides these judicial *panchayats* formally constituted as such, it has been found that whenever a village council is set up for any purpose under the time-honoured title of *panchayat*, it almost instinctively shows a tendency to settle disputes among the villagers. The ideas of *panchayat* and arbitration are so closely linked together in the minds of the people that such an

[1] October 2, 1912.

[2] *Punjab Gazette*, 1912, part v, p. 190.

assumption of power does not appear to them strange or irregular. The best instance is that of village co-operative credit societies. These societies, as a rule, are based on the principle of unlimited liability, so that it is to the interest of each member to see that the other members do not misbehave and land the society in difficulties. It is recognized that litigation often leads to indebtedness, and to check litigation, therefore, becomes an interest of the society. There is an excellent account of this aspect of the co-operative credit movement in Bengal in the last Census Report.[1] It is stated there that in Midnapore alone the societies decided 112 village disputes in a year. "In some societies no member is allowed to go to Court without first consulting the members. . . . In one society a member was fined one rupee for assaulting his aged mother. Another expelled a member for eloping with his neighbour's wife. In . . . it was decided at a general meeting to smoke only tobacco and not cigarettes—the cigarette smoker was to be fined. In another society two members were fined five rupees each for mortgaging their land surreptitiously and their loans were called in." The following incident which occurred in a co-operative credit society in the United Provinces was reported by the Registrar. "The *panchayat* enjoined on one Fakhr-ud-din, who was kept under police surveillance owing to his previous convictions, to be of good behaviour for one year, after which he would be enrolled as one of its members. Fakhr-ud-din did so, and he has now become a member on condition of his committing no more offences in future, and I find he is now quietly carrying on his agricultural pursuits like a good tenant."[2] Similarly it used to be noted years ago in Bengal that village police *panchayats* (*chaukidari panchayats*) sometimes acted as arbitrators in village

[1] *Census of India*, 1911, vol. v, part i, p. 490.
[2] *Report, Co-operative Societies, United Provinces*, 1907–8, App. B, para. 13.

offences which resulted in some districts in a perceptible decrease in criminal cases, though, of course, this was not included by law within their powers.[1] Their duty under the law was to report offences and not to arbitrate.

16. Village *panchayats* of the old communal type, not organized in any way either for judicial or for non-judicial purposes, but with the traditional, unorganized methods of proceeding, have been found, though rarely, in certain places within the past thirty years. It was reported in Bengal in 1880, by a judicial officer in the district of Dinajpore, that "remnants of the old system of village *panchayats* are still to be seen there, and that not a few differences are adjudicated upon by those agencies."[2] The Chief Commissioner of Burma said in 1887: "The custom of referring disputes of all kinds to village elders is deeply rooted in the nature of the people, and it still prevails to a considerable extent notwithstanding the introduction of definite laws and codes."[3] In the North-West Provinces a special officer who was deputed to inquire into the existence of *panchayats* reported in 1892 that "there was ample evidence to show that the custom of appealing to the leading men of the villages in the case of disputes was still alive and in force, though in different degrees in different localities, being at its lowest ebb in Oudh and the eastern districts of the North-West Provinces, and being followed to a great extent in the Western districts."[4] An English honorary magistrate in Chota Nagpur, in giving evidence before the Decentralization Commission in 1907, said: "I use the *panchayats* largely myself. . . . In cases which can be

[1] *Report, Criminal Justice, Lower Provinces of Bengal*, 1881, p. 4; *Ibid.*, 1885, p. 5.

[2] *Ibid.*, 1880, p. 5.

[3] *Report, Civil Justice, Lower Burma*, 1887, Orders of Chief Commissioner, para. 1.

[4] Quoted in North-West Provinces Legislative Council by the Hon. J. Deas, August 13, 1892.

compromised, I advise the parties to lay the matter before a *panchayat*; the *panchayat* meets outside my office, and they generally settle matters more satisfactorily than I could myself."[1] So the chairman of the Assam Tea Planters' Association said: "I use the *panchayats* largely myself in my work, and I always try and let the *coolies* settle their disputes by their own *panchayats*, because they do it more satisfactorily than I would."[2] "The *mels* or *panchayats* of Assam still carry on a fair amount of informal judicial work."[3] And in Madras in 1909 the collector of Tanjore, in explanation of a fall in the institution of regular suits among villagers, reported that there was a tendency among the rural population "to settle their affairs without resorting to any tribunal."[4]

17. It is interesting to recall a memorandum written by Sir Henry Maine thirty-five years ago on the question of reviving the old village *panchayat*.[5] It was written in answer to a report on the condition of India by Mr. James Caird, who was sent out from England as a member of the Indian Famine Commission of 1880. Mr. Caird, on his return to England, sent a report[6] to Lord Salisbury, who was then Secretary of State for India, setting out his views on the causes of agricultural distress in India. In his opinion, the decay of village institutions was one of the chief causes. On this Sir Henry Maine wrote: "I am the last person to deny interest and value to the village community and its characteristic institutions. It is a primitive, natural, social organism. It seems to have been continued longer among the Hindus than among other communities of the same race by the prevailing anarchy of the country, and doutless they owed it to some rudimentary administration of justice when no Government existed

[1] Dr. Andrew Campbell.
[2] William Skinner.
[3] *Imperial Gazetteer of India*, vol. vi, p. 83.
[4] *Report, Civil Justice, Madras*, 1909, para. 3.
[5] *Life and Speeches of Sir Henry Maine*, Murray, 1892, pp. 425–6.
[6] *Report on the Condition of India*, 1879.

outside the village capable of giving authority to court or judge. But to abolish the tribunals which have now existed in parts of British India for more than a century, and to go back to the village courts, is to follow the precedent set the other day by the Chinese Government, which, having got possession of the only railway in the country, proceeded to take up the rails and destroy the earthworks. You may dismantle the road, but you cannot prevent travellers from again wasting their time and becoming footsore. You may revive the village courts, but you will inevitably resuscitate the barbarism which went with them. Speaking generally, he who would bring to life again one of these barbarous institutions is placed in the following dilemma : either he must connive at many of their accompaniments which are condemned by modern morality and modern civilization, or in the attempt to give them a new character, he must so transmute them that they cannot be distinguished in any sensible degree from the modern institutions by which civilization has superseded them."

18. Nobody will now question the enormous contribution by Sir Henry Maine to the study of the village community in India. We owe it to him, to the immense width and variety of his learning and to his comprehensive outlook, that the Indian village community has been set in its right perspective in relation to the general progress of human society. But it is well known that the information on which Maine worked must have been necessarily defective, and that some of his specific conclusions were largely coloured by his preconceptions. Most of the *District Gazetteers* in the different provinces, which now constitute our most valuable storehouse of information, were compiled since his time ; and the great commissions of inquiry beginning with the Famine Commission of 1880 and ending with the Decentralization Commission of 1907, have all been held since he left India. It is, therefore,

permissible to suggest that much value need not be attached to Maine's criticism on village courts. Mr. Caird in his report, which contains some rather sweeping generalizations, does not conceal his strong prepossession in favour of the old village community, but it does not appear from a perusal of the report that he asked for any abolition of existing tribunals. He asked only for a recognition of village *panchayats*. It is not clear that village *panchayats* were so irrevocably wedded to ideas "condemned by modern civilization" that such a recognition would necessarily bring back with it a tide of "barbarism." They had no codes of law, either substantive or adjectival, in which whatever ideas they had could be embodied in any fixed form, nor, so far as we may make out, had they any written record of their decisions spreading over many generations. They merely trusted to their native wit, to experience, to a shrewd sense of passing events, to a fleeting memory of what their fathers did. They were plain men of the world, unsophisticated by much education, who, in spite of frequent failures, tried by whatever means lay in their power to heal quarrels and make peace, and knew by bitter experience how good a thing it was for brethren to dwell together in unity. That the revival of such an institution should bring back with it any fixed system of revolting ideas is incomprehensible. It is also not defensible to say that in any attempt to revive them, they would necessarily be so transmuted as not to be distinguishable from the regular tribunals. These tribunals deal with the formal suit, with the quarrel fitted up in all the trappings of the law and made to look bigger than it really is. They do not and cannot go to the root of the quarrel and settle it before men waste the fortunes of a lifetime on it. That even after the first decade of the twentieth century they can set about their work without putting the village back into barbarism and, at the same time, in essentially different ways from the legally constituted tribunals, is rendered probable by the story of the co-operative credit movement in recent years.

19. We must now go back to the village headman and notice his judicial powers as organized by law. Madras again takes the lead. His position here as a civil court was first formulated by a regulation of 1816,[1] which was modified in respect of certain matters of jurisdiction by an Act of 1883.[2] These two enactments were superseded by a later Act in 1889, the *Madras Village Courts Act*,[3] which to this day has remained the law on the subject. The matters triable by a village headman are confined to claims for money and for personal property; other matters are entirely outside his jurisdiction. The value of the claim must not exceed twenty rupees ordinarily, but if the parties execute a written consent to it, the limit may be raised to two hundred rupees. The village headman, who is styled the *munsif* when he acts in this capacity, is required to write down the proceedings of his court, and in doing so he may demand the assistance of the village accountant. The watchman acts as the messenger of the court, serving summonses, notices and orders, and is employed by the headman in seizing, selling, and delivering movable properties attached under the Act. The decision of the village headman may be revised by a *district munsif* if sufficiently serious grounds are shown. The *district munsif* has also the power, if any of the parties desire it, to transfer a case from one village court to another, or from a village court to his own court. Moreover, the jurisdiction of a village headman in the matters which he is empowered to try is not an exclusive jurisdiction, but concurrent with that of a *district munsif*—that is to say, it is left entirely to a litigant whether he takes a case to a village headman or to a *district munsif*.

20. It will be noticed, then, that the village

[1] Reg. iv. of 1816. [2] Act iv. of 1883. [3] Act i. of 1889.

headman as a regular civil court has been in existence in Madras for very nearly a century, and it is instructive to take note of the estimates which have been formed of his work from time to time. The figures which are available as regards the actual outturn of work show fluctuations now and then, but there has been on the whole a fairly steady rate of progress. The first year after the passing of the Regulation (1817–18), the number of suits instituted in village courts was from about 8,000 to 10,000. In 1883 it it was 49,000. There was an increase in the extent of the headman's jurisdiction in 1883, and from that year on to 1889, when the present Act was passed, the annual average was somwhere about 68,000.[1] The figure for 1911 of suits disposed of by village headmen was roughly 96,000.[2] As pointed out above, the course of progress has not been uniform, but has shown more or less frequent ups and downs. The number for 1911, for example, shows a fall compared with the previous year, and sometime before, and for a year or two after, 1889 there was a somewhat unaccountable fall in the institution of suits. Neither the steady general progress nor the fluctuations have been accounted for in any really satisfying manner. The reports often appear to take shelter in generalizations which are disproved by specific facts or in circumstances of an obviously casual and sporadic character. The question is worth fuller investigation, since it touches two matters of great moment to the rural population. In the first place, a considerable amount of rural litigation is in the hands of village headmen, and the amount and character of rural litigation is a good index to the economic and moral condition of the ryots. In the second place, the confidence reposed in the headmen and their judicial competence, which these figures bring

[1] Speech by the Hon. J. Deas in North-West Provinces Legislative Council, August 13, 1892.
[2] *Report, Civil Justice, Madras*, 1911, para. 7.

out, are of obvious interest in any attempt to improve or modify village local government.

21. A point of great interest in a study of these figures is the fact that the village headman and the *district munsif* have a concurrent jurisdiction. So there might be a simultaneous increase of cases in the two kinds of courts, or a simultaneous fall, or a rise in one and a fall in the other. In each case a different explanation would have to be sought, mainly turning on the point whether the change is due to a rise or fall in the amount of general litigation or in the confidence and popularity inspired by village courts. A great excess in the number of cases before *district munsifs* over the number in village courts which took place in the early years of the working of the system was thus explained by the Court of *Sadr Adalat* in 1829: "It would be going too far to say that the disproportion between the work before the village and that brought before the *district munsifs*, is attributable solely and exclusively to the preference manifested by the natives to the courts of the latter, because from the information before the Court, it would appear that a disinclination to undertake the office of *munsif* prevails to a great extent among the heads of villages, and that in point of fact comparatively few willingly perform, and many have positively refused to perform, the duties assigned to them. This, of course, may be supposed to have contributed largely to the institution of so many petty suits before the *district munsifs*; but in the provinces most of the petty suits which come before a legal tribunal are those in which the moneyed interest, or the village and district bankers sue the ryots and cultivators, who are usually the defendants. In such suits the village judge, however just, must be liable to a bias in favour of his fellow-cultivators. It is therefore natural that the opposite party should prefer the district to the village court, more especially as the very distance of the former, by increasing the inconvenience of litigation to

the party sued, may be held out by the suitor *in terrorem* to his other debtors in order to induce payment of their just debt without recourse to law. Whilst therefore the village *munsif* may compose many village feuds, and allay many feuds between ryot and ryot before they ripen into a lawsuit, the judges are of opinion that when recourse to law is decided on, the suitor, from a knowledge of his bias in favour of his fellow-cultivators or from his influence having already been exercised against the suit, is inclined to prefer another tribunal." [1]

22. An increase of cases in village courts which is not accompanied by a corresponding decrease in cases of the same character in *district munsifs'* courts would indicate that village courts have not succeeded in what is accounted to be one of their primary purposes, namely to relieve the regular courts of their ordinary petty work. On this a special officer of the North-West Provinces Government who was deputed by the latter to inquire into the working of the Madras system with a view to its introduction into their own province, offered this explanation (1892): "The disputes they (village courts) decide are, as a rule, those which, on account of the petty interests at stake and the expense and inconvenience involved in prosecuting them before the regular courts, would never go to those courts at all. It is not, therefore, in the direction of affording any tangible relief to the regular courts that the institution of village *munsifs* in Madras has been effectual. The work they have done and the benefit they have been to the people lie in this, that through their means thousands of wrongs have been redressed which the machinery of the regular courts was too cumbrous and too costly to remedy, and which would presumably in most instances have remained unadjusted." [2] Since the

[1] *Report of Select Committee*, 1832, App. (2), Jud. iv.

[2] Speech by the Hon. J. Deas, North-West Provinces Legislative Council, August 13, 1892.

above was written, there has been in the Madras Presidency an enormous expansion in general civil litigation. And the Madras Government, in their latest review of judicial administration (1913), record the "significant" fact that the increase per cent. in the number of suits before *district munsifs* of the value of 20 rupees and under (which are the suits which might also be taken to village courts according to the pleasure of the party) was much less than the increase in suits above 20 rupees.[1] The significance is that the existence of village courts must have drawn off a considerable proportion of the general increase in civil litigation which might otherwise have gone to swell the regular courts.

23. The cause of the steady decline which was noticed in the work of village courts for a few years before and after 1889 formed the subject of an interesting argument between the Madras High Court and the Madras Government, in which it must be confessed that, in spite of their daily practice in the disputations of the law, their Lordships of the High Court did not exactly cover themselves with glory. The position of the latter was this: "With the development of the habit of travelling, which naturally ensues on the increased facilities of communication, the expansion of trade, and the general progress of the country, the isolation of the village community is destroyed, and the patriarchal influence of the headman consequently weakened, while at the same time the accessibility of the regular courts becomes more widely known. The spread of education, too, has increased the number of authorized Legal Practitioners and others who live by the law, and it is to the interest of these classes to promote recourse to the regular courts instead of the primitive village tribunals. Moreover, there has been a marked

[1] *Report, Civil Justice, Madras*, 1913, Orders of Government.

improvement of late years in the supervision exercised over the village courts, and by the introduction of Act i. of 1889 such increased powers of control over village *munsifs* are provided as must doubtless make these officers more circumspect in their conduct and less prone than of old to abuse their authority in the interest of those classes who must frequently have occasion to claim the aid of the civil law."[1] It fell to the lot of the Madras Government to throw its mantle over the Legal Practitioner and save him from the attack of the High Court—a very chivalrous thing to have done, seeing that their normal relations have never been marred by any excessive love! The argument of education, of increase in communications, and in the number of Legal Practitioners somewhat broke down, because, as the Government pointed out, the decline in the work of village courts was most manifest in the least developed districts of the Presidency, such as Kurnool and Cuddapah, and scarcely noticed in such advanced districts as Tanjore and Madura. The Government themselves pointed to a proportionate decrease in petty litigation of all kinds during the period in question as the cause of the decline.[2] And in another connection they drew attention to a fact, which perhaps will bear fuller inquiry, that village courts seem to be more popular in the Tamil than in the Telugu parts of the Presidency.[3]

24. In Bombay the appointment of village headmen as civil judicial officers was sanctioned in 1879 by the Deccan Agriculturists' Relief Act.[4] This Act was passed in consequence of a serious riot which took place in certain districts of the Bombay Presidency to resist the exactions of village money-

[1] *Report, Civil Justice, Madras*, 1889, para. 17.
[2] *Ibid.*, Orders of Government, para. 4.
[3] *Report, Criminal Justice, Madras*, 1889, Orders of Government, para. 4.
[4] Act xvii. of 1879.

lenders. The agricultural scarcity which prevailed at the time made these exactions felt with exceptional acuteness. It is interesting to look upon this riot as a rough sort of protest which the patient Indian villager is sometimes driven to make when the social system in which he lives works too hard on him. Most village riots in India are sporadic occurrences, in which the impulse of the moment is the prime factor, but this one was of a different kind. It was of the same character as the riot which occurred in some districts of the Madras Presidency in 1896 as a protest against the methods of criminal tribes engaged privately as village policemen. Their significance lies in this, that things must have got pretty intolerable when the villager was induced to break through his immemorable patience in revolt against a system which has ever been part of his social life. The unique feature of the Bombay Act is that along with investing village headmen with judicial powers there is also a system of what are called Conciliators. "Their functions are, on the application of either of the parties to a dispute, to endeavour to induce them to agree either to a compromise or a reference to arbitration. If the Conciliators succeed, they may send the settlement arrived at, or the reference agreed to, to the Court to be filed, when it has the effect of a decree or reference to arbitration under the Civil Procedure Code. If they fail, they grant a certificate to that effect, and either party can then seek redress in court; but without such certificate no suit to which any agriculturist residing within any local area for which a Conciliator has been appointed is a party, may be entertained in a Civil Court." [1] Some other differences from the Madras system may be noticed. The jurisdiction of the headmen is limited to suits of ten rupees in value, and is an exclusive jurisdiction

---

[1] *Bombay Administration Report*, 1911–12, para. 27.

not concurrent with that of the regular courts. The matters triable, though generally the same as in Madras, are slightly more limited in range.

25. The application of the Act was originally confined to select areas in four districts, but since August, 1905, it has been extended to the whole Presidency. The Act has not been worked with any conspicuous measure of success so far. The total number of village headmen who exercised judicial powers under it in 1910 was only 194, and the number of Conciliators 644.[1] The figures for 1903—that is, two years before the general extension of the Act—were 92 and 256.[2] During the earlier years, the special judge who was in charge of the Act remarked from his observation that the cases which went to the new village courts were not due so much to a diversion of existing litigation from the regular courts as to the creation of new litigation.[3] The fact would admit of two explanations: either, as was pointed out with regard to Madras in paragraph 22, that the new litigation represented wrongs which were honestly felt but were suppressed for want of courts cheap, prompt, and near at hand, or that it was merely the result of a frivolous and vexatious litigiousness. The Conciliators have, on the whole, come in for a great deal of criticism. The complaint has been throughout on the question of the *personnel*. One of the earlier reports pointed out that the appointments were made too hastily, and that sufficient time was not allowed for the selection of right men.[4] "In theory the Conciliator is a local magnate who gives much time to the noble occupation of peace-making. In practice he is often a man of no influence or ability or energy, and he merely takes up the post by way of increasing his own importance."[5] A district judge,

[1] *Bombay Administration Report*, 1911–2, para. 27.
[2] *Report, Civil Justice, Bombay*, 1903, para. 10.
[3] *Ibid.*, 1880, para. 19.
[4] *Ibid.*, para. 22.
[5] *Ibid.*, 1910, para. 7.

who was on the whole sympathetic towards the principles of the Act, gave the following account of how it has been received, which may be quoted for what it is worth. "Lawyers dislike it, as it decreases their work. Lenders object to it because they are no longer sure of getting exorbitant interest and compelling the cultivator to give up his land. And the cultivator thinks that the Act has decreased his credit."[1]

26. In the United Provinces village courts are set up in pursuance of an Act passed in 1892.[2] But the first appointments of headmen were not actually made till three years after. The character of the system mainly follows that of Madras, and on the whole a fair measure of success may be said to have attended its working hitherto. The number of headmen exercising powers of civil justice in 1913 was 305, and they tried between them nearly 11,000 cases.[3] A few years ago the High Court of Allahabad said: "It is true that the village courts failed to check the increase of litigation in regular courts. . . . But this is not a sufficient ground for believing that the undoubtedly large amount of work done is wasted. That substantial justice is done may be inferred from the fact that only 78 revisions were filed against 1,231 decisions in contested cases, and of these only 14 were successful. But the system has not yet been fully accepted by the people, and therefore the greatest care is necessary to keep up its credit by appointing only thoroughly qualified men as village *munsifs*."[4] In Burma headmen receive their judicial powers under the Burma Village Act, 1907, which amended and consolidated the previous enactments in Lower and Upper Burma. In 1913 there were in Upper Burma

[1] *Report, Civil Justice, Bombay*, 1910, para. 7.
[2] United Provinces, Act iii. of 1892.
[3] *Report, Civil Justice, North-West Provinces*, 1913, para. 9.
[4] *Ibid.*, 1906, para. 10.

598 headmen empowered to try civil cases. Of these, however, only 278 made use of their powers, and they decided 2,162 cases.[1] The disproportion between the number of those who are empowered and those who actually exercise their power has been frequently commented on in recent years as a disappointing feature. But as it was expressed in a report of 1910, "Public opinion is strong in Burman villages, and headmen may be trusted to do justice in petty village disputes."[2]

27. Village headmen possess also powers of criminal justice by law. In Madras they exercise these powers under two old Regulations—one of 1816[3] and the other of 1821.[4] The cases triable by them as magistrates are petty cases of abuse, assault, and theft, and the punishments which they are authorized to inflict on convicted persons are imprisonment in the village *choultry*[5] for a term not exceeding twelve hours, or to put them in the stocks for not over six hours. This latter punishment is confined to lower castes upon whom "it may not be improper to inflict so degrading a punishment." Christians and Muhammadans have had to be specially mentioned as classes whom it would be improper to punish in this way.[6] In Bombay village headmen are appointed magistrates under a provision in the Village Police Act, 1867. Ordinarily their powers are limited to petty assault and abuse, but headmen may be specially selected for enhanced powers and authorized to try various other petty offences such as mischief, theft, and nuisance. The punishment awarded in ordinary trials is imprisonment in the village *chaunri*[5] for a period not exceeding twenty-four hours, but when

[1] *Report, Civil Justice, Upper Burma*, 1913, para. 17.
[2] *Ibid.*, 1910, para. 14.
[3] Reg. xi. of 1816, secs. 10 and 14.
[4] Reg. iv. of 1821, sec. 6.
[5] Village meeting-house.
[6] *Madras Village Officers' Manual*, 1913, ch. iii, para. 44.

selected headmen exercise extraordinary powers they may inflict a fine extending to five rupees, or in default, imprisonment for forty-eight hours. Somewhat similar powers are conferred on village headmen in Burma under rules framed in pursuance of the Village Act, 1907. The Police Commission (1902–3) made this remark on the system of village magistrates generally: "In Madras the Commission have had before them strong evidence that the powers of the headmen in disposing of petty criminal cases may safely be enlarged to some extent. It would not, perhaps, be expedient to give them powers to sentence to longer terms of imprisonment than at present allowed, for that involves the housing, guarding, and dieting of prisoners, but enhancement of their power of fine might well be considered. This enhancement of powers might be carried out in this province and elsewhere on the principle of sec. 15 of the Bombay Village Police Act (viii. of 1867), namely, that enhanced powers may be conferred on selected headmen. This would serve to encourage others to good work, as the experience of Burma has shown. In provinces where the custom of employing headmen in the disposal of petty cases does not exist, the Commission would strongly urge that it should be experimentally introduced. It is in accordance with native custom and sentiment. Village opinion forms a strong check on the resident headmen. It would relieve the people from police interference in petty cases."[1]

28. Before concluding this chapter it is necessary to refer briefly to local tribunals connected with castes and tribes, which, though not strictly village institutions, are yet engaged in carrying on a considerable amount of informal judicial work among the rural population. A caste is often just a section of a village community, and sometimes includes in its organization similar

[1] *Report*, ch. iii.

sections of other communities. A tribe generally represents an organization which extends over more villages than one, and the administrative notion of a village in a tribal region is the area occupied by a sub-division of a tribe. A clear-cut distinction between "caste," "tribe," and "village community" may be hazardous, but the characteristic principles of each may be roughly expressed thus. The bond of a *caste* is *occupation*, of a tribe *kinship*, and of a village *locality*.

29. The organ by which a caste administers justice is the caste *panchayat*, similar in constitution to a village *panchayat* except that the membership is restricted to the particular caste. The usual offences with which they concern themselves relate to the social laws of the caste, especially offences of a domestic kind, not generally recognizable by the regular courts. But these do not altogether exhaust the jurisdiction of caste tribunals, and interesting cases have been noted, even in recent years, of castes encroaching on what is properly the work of the courts, sometimes to help and sometimes to hinder the regular administration of justice. In criminal matters they are found to try small offences of theft and abuse, and have also been known to handle more serious offences like murder. Their civil jurisdiction is exercised in such matters as the recovery of debts, inheritance, and the partition of joint-family property. The main sanction of a caste tribunal is the fear of excommunication, which is seldom, if ever, lightly regarded. But before this extreme step is taken, fines, compensations, the feeding of the caste, some act of degradation such as carrying a shoe on one's head, are prescribed as punishments.[1]

30. Tribal institutions for the administration of justice are found in the North-West Frontier Province, Baluchistan and Sind. The characteristics of the different tribes who inhabit these provinces are not

[1] See chapters on "Caste Government" in the *Provincial Reports of the Census of India*, 1911.

always the same. The *Pathans*, for example, on the Afghan frontier, are a more democratic body than the *Baluchis*, and are not organized under a common leader like the latter. But in every tribe, the elders or leaders of clans have great influence, and much of the work of administering justice is done through them. Councils of elders, called *Jirgas*, have now been formally constituted under the Frontier Crimes Regulation, 1901, and the Sind Frontier Regulation, 1892. The nomination of the members, who number in each case three or more, is made by, or under the direction of, the Deputy Commissioner, and their primary purpose is the settlement of offences in which there is sufficient evidence for moral certainty but not for a judicial conviction. The local knowledge and authority of the elders are to supply the lack of legal evidence. The Council, in fact, is to supplement, not to supersede, the regular courts. The matters on which a Deputy Commissioner may make a reference to a Council of Elders are those which he believes likely to cause "a blood-feud, or murder or culpable homicide not amounting to murder, or mischief, or a breach of the peace"; [1] and their findings are carried out by him if they are not opposed "to good conscience or public policy." [2] The compensation of the aggrieved party, and the distribution of the obligation to pay among the relatives and fellow-tribesmen of the offender, is the real object of a tribal council. But the award of imprisonment instead has become usual, though it is regarded by those who have experience of the system as an undesirable exercise of power. The rates of compensation which now prevail by tribal custom are about 1,000 rupees for a person killed, and from 100 rupees to 300 rupees for a person seriously wounded.[3] In Baluchistan a Central Tribal Council called a *Shahi Jirga* is held half-yearly at the head-

[1] Reg. iii. of 1901, sec. 8. [2] Sec. 9.
[3] *Report, Criminal Justice, North-West Frontier Province*, 1913.

quarters of the Government for the decision of inter-tribal disputes. The weaknesses of the *Jirga* system appear to be principally the difficulty of getting impartial competent men to sit on them, and the temptation for magistrates and police officers to transfer to the tribes the responsibility for inquiring into cases which are more properly within their jurisdiction.

APPENDIX

RESOLUTION OF THE GOVERNMENT OF INDIA ON LOCAL SELF-GOVERNMENT ISSUED IN MAY, 1915, PARAGRAPHS 37, 38 AND 39

37. THE Commission[1] recommended the constitution and development of village *panchayats* possessed with certain administrative powers, with jurisdiction in petty civil and criminal cases, and financed by a portion of the land cess, special grants, receipts from village cattle pounds and markets, and small fees on civil suits. This proposal, favourably commended by the Government of India, who expressed their readiness to acquiesce in some form of permissive taxation, if need be, has in general been sympathetically received. The practical difficulties are, however, felt to be very great in many parts of India. The Government of Burma and the Chief Commissioner of the Central Provinces deprecate the introduction of a system, which, in their judgment, is alien to the customs of the people, and will not command public confidence. Other Governments are willing to experiment, but on different lines. The Punjab Government has already established *panchayats* for civil cases only and of a voluntary character. Sir Leslie Porter, when officiating as Lieutenant-Governor of the United Provinces, expressed his willingness to entrust selected *panchayats* with criminal as well as civil jurisdiction. The Madras

[1] *The Royal Commission on Decentralization in India*, 1907.

Government are desirous of experimenting in the establishment of *panchayats*, but consider that action should be confined for the present to the encouragement of voluntary self-contained organisms, independent of statutory sanction and consisting of village elders conferring together for common village purposes. So far as judicial functions are concerned they are content to rely on the provisions of the Madras Village *Panchayats* Regulation, 1816, and the Madras Village Courts Act, 1888, which authorize the assembling of *panchayats* and the convening of village bench courts for the settlement of particular civil suits on the application of the parties, and to encourage the operation of these enactments wherever practicable. The Governments of Bengal and of Behar and Orissa are of opinion that their existing laws sufficiently provide for the establishment of *panchayats*, with administrative duties, while powers to dispose of criminal cases could be given under the existing Acts dealing with these matters. The Chief Commissioner of Assam has expressed his readiness to develop village government, and the Local Self-Government Bill which has recently passed the Legislative Council of that province permits the constitution of village authorities, the grant of funds by Local Boards and from other sources, and the delegation of minor powers of local control. The whole question has now been raised again in the discussions contained in the report of the Bengal District Administration Committee, 1913–14.

38. The Commission recognized that any policy of establishing *panchayats* would be the work of many years, would require great care and discretion, and much patience and judicious discrimination between the circumstances of different villages. The Government of India desire that where any practical scheme can be worked out in co-operation with the people concerned, full experiment should be made on lines approved by the local Government or Administration

concerned. Throughout the greater part of India the word "*panchayat*" is familiar. The lower castes commonly have voluntarily constituted *panchayats*, to whom they allow quasi-judicial authority in social matters. The more artificial administrative committees, such as *chaukidari panchayats*, local fund unions, and village sanitation and education committees, and, in places even village *panchayats*, already exist. The spread of co-operative societies and distribution of Government advances in time of famine and scarcity on joint security are educative influences. Village tribunals for the disposal of petty civil suits have got beyond the experimental stage in some places and are in the experimental stage in others. There is, therefore, some material with which to build. The Government of India agree, however, with the view prominently brought forward by the Bengal District Administration Committee that much will depend on the local knowledge and personality of the officers who may be selected to introduce any scheme.

39. With this general commendation, the Government of India are content to leave the matter in the hands of local Governments and Administrations. They are disposed to consider that the following general principles indicate the lines on which advance is most likely to be successful :—

(1) The experiments should be made in selected villages or areas larger than a village, where the people in general agree.

(2) Legislation, where necessary, should be permissive and general. The powers and duties of *panchayats*, whether administrative or judicial, need not and, indeed, should not be identical in every village.

(3) In areas where it is considered desirable to confer judicial as well as administrative functions upon *panchayats* the same body should exercise both functions,

(4) Existing village administrative committees, such as village sanitation and education committees, should be merged in the village *panchayats* where these are established.

(5) The jurisdiction of *panchayats* in judicial cases should ordinarily be permissive, but in order to provide inducement to litigants reasonable facilities might be allowed to persons wishing to have their cases decided by *panchayats*. For instance, court fees, if levied, should be small, technicalities in procedure should be avoided, and possibly a speedier execution of decrees permitted.

(6) Powers of permissive taxation may be conferred on *panchayats*, where desired, subject to the control of the local Government or Administration, but the development of the *panchayat* system should not be prejudiced by an excessive association with taxation.

(7) The relations of *panchayats* on the administrative side with other administrative bodies should be clearly defined. If they are financed by district or sub-district boards, there can be no objection to some supervision by such boards.

LIST OF REFERENCES

Abdur Rahim. Muhammadan Jurisprudence (Tagore Law Lectures).

Adam's Reports on Vernacular Education in Bengal and Behar. Long.

Administration Reports, Provincial, Annual.

Anandaranga Pillay, The Private Diary of. Price.

Arbuthnot, Minutes of Sir T. Munro.

Archæological Survey of India, Reports, Annual.

Arthas'āstra. Mysore Review. 1907–9.

Arundel, A. T. Irrigation and Communal Labour in the Madras Presidency.

Baden-Powell, B. H. The Indian Village Community.

" " The Land Systems of British India, 3 vols.

Bhattacharya, Commentaries on the Hindu Law.

Caird, J. Report on the Condition of India.

Calcutta Review. 1900.

Census of India, 1901 and 1911. Reports, General and Provincial.

Central Provinces, Local Rules and Orders.

Chaplin, W. Report on the Deccan.

Co-operative District Conference. Tanjore. 1914. Proceedings.

Co-operative Societies. Reports.

Cox, Sir E. Police and Crime in India.

Decentralization in India, Royal Commission on, 1907. Report and Evidence.

East India Association, Proceedings.

Education Commission, 1882–3. Reports and Evidence.

Education, Reports, Annual Provincial and Quinquennial.

Egypt, Report on Finance, Administration, etc. 1908, 1913.
Elphinstone, M. Report on the Territories Conquered from the Paishwa.
Epigraphia Indica.
Epigraphic Reports, Madras.

Famine Codes.
Famine Commission. 1880. Report and Evidence.
" " 1898. Report.
Famine Reports.
Forest Committee, Madras, 1913. Report and Evidence.

Gazettes, India and Provincial. Supplements containing Government Resolutions and Acts.
Gazetteer of India, Imperial.
Gazetteers, District.

Havell, E. B. Ancient and Mediæval Architecture of India.
Haxthausen, Baron. The Russian Empire. (Translated by R. Fairie.)
Hill, S. C. Yusuf Khan, the Rebel Commandant.
Hindu, The. Madras. Weekly Edition.
Hitopadesa. Francis Johnson.
Holmes, O. W., Jun. The Common Law.
Howell, A. Education in British India.
Hughes, Dictionary of Islam.
Hunter, W. W. Annals of Rural Bengal.

India, Weekly Paper, London.
Irrigation Commission, 1901–3. Report and Evidence.

Jarvis, T. B. Geographical and Statistical Memoir of the Konkun.

Legislative Councils, Imperial and Provincial, Proceedings.
Lely, Sir F. S. Suggestions for the Better Governing of India.
Leroy-Beaulieu. The Empire of the Tsars.

Madras Mail, The Weekly.
Mahabharata (Roy).
Maine, Sir H. S. Ancient Law.
" " Early History of Institutions.

Maine, Sir H. S. Early Law and Custom.
" " Life and Speeches.
" " Village Communities in the East and West.
Maitland, F. W. Township and Borough.
Malcolm, Sir J. Minute on the Administration of the Southern Maratha Country.
Mānava Dharma Sāstra (Jones and Haughton).
Memorandum on the Administration of India during the Past Thirty Years. 1858.
Mitra, A. C. Hindu Law.
Modern Review. Calcutta. 1913.
Morison, Sir T. The Economic Transition in India.
Muir, Sir. W. James Thomason.

Police Commission, 1902–3. Report and Abstract of Evidence as published in Indian newspapers.
Police Committee, Madras, 1902. Statement.
Police in Bengal, Report of the Committee to Consider the Reform of. 1891.
Police in the Madras Presidency, Papers Connected with the Reorganization of, 1859.
Police Regulations in the U.P.
Police Reports, Annual Provincial.
Pollock, Sir F. Maine's Ancient Law.
Pollock and Maitland. History of English Law.
Public Works in the Madras Presidency, Second Report of Commissioners, 1853.

Rām Rāz. Essay on the Architecture of the Hindus.

Sanitary Conferences, All India, Proceedings.
Sanitary Reports, Imperial and Provincial, Annual.
Select Committee on East India Affairs. 1812. Report.
" " " 1831. Proceedings.
Sharp, H. Occasional Reports, I.
Sleeman, Sir W. Rambles and Recollections, 1893.
Smith, V. A. Early History of India. 1914.
South Indian Inscriptions.
Srinivasa raghava Iyengar, Memorandum on the Administration of the Madras Presidency.
S'ukra-Nīti. (Sacred Books of the Hindus.)

Tamilian Antiquary, The.
Temple, R. Report on the Administration of the Government of the Nizam.
Thillai Govindan.
Thurston, E. Castes and Tribes of Southern India.
Trevelyan, E. J. Hindu Family Law.

Village Officers' Manual, Madras.
Vinogradoff, P. The Growth of the Manor.

Webb, S. and B. The Parish and the County.
" " The Story of the King's Highway.
Wilks, Historical Sketches of South India.

INDEX